KT-222-521

Innovations in Nursing Care

A Study of a Change to Patient Centred Care

CLAIRE A. HALE
BA, PhD, SRN, RNT

WITHDRAWN

ACC. No.	CL. *WY 101*
114144	*BAR*
DATE *10/2/89* *20.5.93*	

SOUTH LOTHIAN COLLEGE OF NURSING & MIDWIFERY
ROYAL INFIRMARY, LAURISTON PLACE, EDINBURGH
NAPIER UNIVERSITY

610.7301 HAL

© Crown Copyright

AIMS OF THE SERIES

To encourage the appreciation and dissemination of nursing research by making relevant studies of high quality available to the profession at reasonable cost.

The RCN is very happy indeed to publish this series of research reports. The projects were chosen by the individual research worker and the findings are those of the researcher and relate to the particular subject in the situation in which it was studied. The RCN in accordance with its policy of promoting research awareness among members of the profession commends this series for study but views expressed do not necessarily reflect RCN policy.

ISBN 0–902606–94–8

Published by
The Royal College of Nursing
of the United Kingdom,
Cavendish Square, London, W1M 0AB.

Printed by The Whitefriars Press Ltd., London and Tonbridge

RESEARCH SERIES EDITORIAL BOARD

Chairman

MISS JENNIFER HUNT, BA(Hons), MPhil, SRN, FRCN
Fellow in Quality Assurance Studies
King's Fund College, London

Vice-Chairman

DR. SENGA BOND, BA, MSc, PhD, RGN, FRCN
Lecturer in Nursing Research, Health Care Research Unit,
University of Newcastle upon Tyne

MISS PAT ASHWORTH, MSc, SRN, SCM, FRCN
Senior Lecturer, Department of Nursing and Health Visiting, University of Ulster.

DR. JUNE M. CROWN, MA, MB, B.Chir, MSc, FFCM
District Medical Officer, Bloomsbury Health Authority.

DR. CELIA DAVIES, BA, MA, PhD
Project Officer, United Kingdom Central Council for Nursing, Midwifery and Health Visiting.

DR. PAULINE FIELDING, BSc(Hons), PhD, RGN
Director of Nursing Services, Whipps Cross Hospital, London.

MISS MARGARET D. GREEN, MA(Ed), BA(Hons), SRN, RNT
Director of Education, Royal College of Nursing.

DR. JILL MACLEOD CLARK, BSc, PhD, SRN
Lecturer in Nursing Studies, Chelsea College, University of London.

DR. ALISON J. TIERNEY, BSc(SocScNurs), PhD, RGN
Director, Nursing Research Unit, Department of Nursing Studies, University of Edinburgh.

DR. BARBARA WADE, BEd, PhD, SRN
Director, The Daphne Heald Research and Development Unit, Royal College of Nursing.

This research monograph was accepted for publication by the previous Research Series Editorial Board

Series Editor: MISS FRANCIS S. BECK, MA, SRN, RNT

Production: MISS VALERIE O'CONNOR, SRN

Contents

List of Tables

List of Figures

Acknowledgements

This study would not have been possible without the help of many nurses, midwives, patients and doctors of the maternity hospital where the study was carried out. They cannot all be named individually but I would like to extend a special thanks to Miss Hazel Millar, Mrs Marjorie Flemming and Dr. David Warrell.

I would like to thank my supervisors Dr. A. J. Berry of the Manchester Business School, and Professor Baroness McFarlane of Llandaff, of the Department of Nursing at Manchester University who both gave me considerable support and encouragement during the research. Many friends and colleagues helped at some point in the study but I am particularly grateful to Dr. Valerie Hillier and Colin Ashcroft of the Computation Unit of Manchester University Medical School.

I am grateful to the Department of Health who funded the research study through their Nursing Research Training Fellowship scheme, and to Dr. Joyce Prince the Nursing Officer (Research). Finally I would like to thank Marie Loftus who so patiently typed the manuscript for this volume and my husband Jack Hale for his encouragement and support both during the research study itself and the preparation of this manuscript.

Preface

This study by Claire Hale was undertaken while she was working in the Department of Nursing of the University of Manchester as a DHSS sponsored research student. It is an attempt to examine the effects of changing the work organisation of a ward from task assignment to a patient centred method.

The practice of nursing is fashioned by the underlying system of values and assumptions held by nurses about nursing care. These are derived partly from the society in which they work but also from the collective values of members of the profession. Lanara (1976) has traced professional values which have their origins in early Greek culture and Byzantine Christianity, but the history of nursing is a rich tapestry of both enduring and changing value systems. Many of the more recent slogans, (total patient care, holistic care, patient centred care and so on) are expressions of values about the nature of the patient and nursing.

Three theses completed in the Department of Nursing of the University of Manchester touch very directly on nurse values. Kratz (1974) in analysing the care given to stroke patients in the community demonstrated that care which was 'focussed' because the objectives and methods were clearly appreciated was valued above care which nurses identified less clearly. Kappeli (1984) demonstrated four different types of professional orientation to meeting the self care needs of the elderly. These were dependent on the professional values that the nurses studied held in respect of the elderly, the nurse-patient relationship and the nature of the professional task. Johnson (1983) in an MSc thesis demonstrated that the values of student nurses changed in their three years of training.

In recent years there has been a strong professional orientation towards the value of individualised patient care. It is a value which underpins the use of Nursing Process in the practice of nursing and is the foundation of our present approach to nursing education. The value placed on individualised rather than routinised approaches to patient care plans owes much to the society in which we live. The views held of the nature of the human person (the patient) prize his uniqueness, independence, dignity, right to freedom and self determination. Psychological theories which stress individual differences underline this view. Other cultures may place a greater emphasis on the value of the group and interdependence. Whatever model of nursing we use incorporates assumptions and values about the nature of the human person in the view they take of the patient or client. It is salutory to make these values explicit. For instance, the self care model is strongly individualistic in its view of the person and stresses the value of independence.

As we adapt the delivery of nursing care to incorporate the developing value system of the profession, it is wise to examine the outcome of changes, to question whether care reflecting a changed value system meets patient needs any more effectively or if it contributes anything more to the job satisfaction of nurses. Claire Hale's study is an attempt at such an examination. Because of my assumptions about the nature of the needs of the individual I found the results of this study surprising and a challenge to re-examine my assumptions and find explanations. The value of the individual is so strongly held in nursing that even in task assigned care there may be elements of individualised care.

Claire Hale examines the research design and methods for their adequacy and looks at the implications of her findings for practice. I believe the study is valuable, because it teaches us to test the values and assumptions which we prize. It should give us pause for thought about what we teach as self evident fact and it opens up many questions for further study. It also teaches us some humility about drawing conclusions from one study and gives an example of a researcher examining her work retrospectively to evaluate the effectiveness of her method.

McFARLANE OF LLANDAFF,
Professor and Head of the Department of Nursing,
University of Manchester

REFERENCES

LANARA V. A. (1976). Philosophy of Nursing and Current Nursing Problems. *Internat. Nurs. Review,* Vol. 23, No. 2
KRATZ C. R. (1974). *Problems of Care of the Long-term Sick in the Community with Particular Reference to Patients with Stroke.* Unpublished PhD thesis, University of Manchester
KAPPELI S. (1984). *Towards a Practice Theory of the Relationships of Self-care Needs, Nursing Needs and Nursing Care in the Hospitalized Elderly.* Unpublished PhD thesis, University of Manchester.
JOHNSON M. (1983). *Values Affecting Decision Making in Nursing.* Unpublished MSc thesis, University of Manchester.

Introduction

That nursing care should be organised to meet the needs of patients is obvious. What is less obvious is exactly how this can be achieved when the situation is not one nurse/one patient, but a small number of nurses for a large number of patients. It becomes even more complicated when we have a situation where the care is given in an institution, where not all the 'nurses' are fully qualified, and where the patients have a variety of individual physical, psychological and social needs.

Traditionally nurses in hospital have concentrated their care on the physical needs of their patients, although in recent years more attention (at least in theory) has been paid to the fact that patients have psychological, social and also spiritual needs. Traditionally nursing care in hospital has been organised around the tasks—the physical tasks, that needed to be done for each patient. Traditionally the nurses in hospital (where not all 'nurses' are fully qualified) organised the delivery of nursing care using an hierarchical approach, with high status tasks (usually the most 'technical' and most administrative) going to high status nurses (usually the most senior and most qualified).

By the 1950s the idea that nursing care in hospitals was too dominated by the task centred/physical care paradigm was gaining some popularity. In 1956 the Royal College of Nursing issued a statement on nursing policy, entitled 'Observations and Objectives' in which they advocated the use of a patient centred approach to care. The particular organisational arrangements and nurse deployment patterns by which it was hoped to achieve the patient centred care became known as "patient allocation". However, despite the claims by some of its advocates that it would improve the satisfaction of patients with their care, and the job satisfaction of the nursing staff, and that it could be implemented with no increase in staff (see Chapter One)—even by the mid 1970s, patient allocation was not widely used as a method of organising nursing work in the United Kingdom.

This study began with the aim of investigating why patient allocation was not more widely used. Since the benefits appeared self evident (what nurse would argue that nursing care which was centred on the individual needs of patients was *not* a good idea), then the answer surely had to lie in personal and organisational factors.

However, in common with many other research studies, it transpired that the research problem was more complex than had originally been anticipated. There was in fact very little research evidence to support the reputed benefits of a system of patient allocation which had been extolled so frequently in the nursing literature—namely that patient satisfaction and staff job satisfaction could be improved.

Nursing care in hospital wards which is organised to meet the individual needs of patients would seem to be highly desirable and intuitively many nurses believe that benefits must arise from this type of care. But, in these days of budget limits and the escalating cost of nursing and medical care, it is no more desirable to base nursing care on intuition, than it is to base it on tradition. We need to know more about how patient centred care can be achieved, how it can be evaluated and exactly what benefits accrue and for whom. Most importantly, we need to know what "patient centred care" *is*.

This study was an attempt to unravel the complexities of introducing and evaluating the benefits of a system of patient allocation. While this study is not able to give all the answers, it is hoped that it may be able to give a pointer to some alternative directions which future researchers may care to take.

Plan of Volume

This volume is based on a research study presented by the author for a PhD degree at Manchester University in 1982 (Metcalf, 1982). The emphasis in this volume is on the design of the study, the findings obtained and the implications of these findings. In the original study, the literature in a number of different areas was reviewed. These areas included, organisation theory and behaviour, the introduction of change, job satisfaction, patient satisfaction and maternity care. It was not possible to include all these areas of literature review in this volume.

Chapter 1 describes the background to the study and some of the specific literature on task and patient allocation is reviewed. Chapter 2 described the conceptual framework and research design and gives a brief account of how the research instruments were developed. Chapter 3 outlines the changes which were introduced into the ward.

The findings of the study are presented in Chapters 4, 5, 6 and 7. The study had four main areas of data collection; an interview study, an observation study, a patient satisfaction study and a job satisfaction study. A chapter is devoted to each separate area. Since such a complex study obviously generated many findings, only a selection could be presented in this volume. Because the research design involved "data triangulation" (Denzin, 1970), with data collected in one area being used to support, or not support, data collected in another area, the findings of each of the four areas of data collection are not discussed in the respective chapters. Instead the findings of all four areas of data collection are drawn together and discussed in the final chapter, Chapter 8.

Terminology

This study took place in a maternity hospital. This caused complications in terminology because many midwives do not like to be referred to as 'nurse' and many mothers and mothers-to-be do not like to be referred to as 'patients'. In this study, the word 'nursing staff' was often used to cover all staff working on the 'research' ward. This included nursing auxiliaries, nursery nurses, student nurses, student/pupil midwives and staff midwives. The word 'mother' was used where possible and appropriate to refer to all the 'patients' in the ward whether or not they had had their baby. Occasionally, however, the 'mothers' were referred to as 'patients' and the 'midwives' were called 'nurses'. I apologise to those whom I have offended.

CHAPTER 1

The Background to the Study

1.1 The Aim of the Study

The purpose of this research study was to introduce and examine the effects of a change in the method of organising the delivery of nursing care in a ward of a maternity hospital. Prior to the study, the organisation of the delivery of nursing care in the ward chosen for the research study was considered to be essentially task centred. The change which was to be introduced was a method of organising the delivery of nursing care which was patient centred.

1.2 Task Allocation and Patient Allocation

In 1978 when this study began, two methods of organising the delivery of nursing care were described in the nursing literature; task allocation and patient allocation. Task allocation was used to refer to a method of organising the delivery of nursing care, where the care of patients was reduced to a set of tasks to be performed, for example, baths, observations, mouthcare, dressings, pressure area care. Nurses were allocated to perform certain tasks for all the patients who required them, and the tasks were usually carried out at specified times. Although task allocation could be a very efficient method of "getting the work done", by the mid-nineteen seventies contemporary trends in the care of patients and professional developments in nursing, had affected the acceptability of a system of task allocation as a method of organising the delivery of nursing care. Two of these trends were:

(i) The emphasis on the importance of the psychosocial aspects of illness which had resulted in an emphasis being placed upon the individual needs of those who sought the services of health care personnel; and

(ii) the increasing 'professionalism' of nursing; supporters of which maintained that nurses were not the mere handmaidens of doctors, but were, or should be, able to accept and exercise considerable responsibility, autonomy and discretion, in their own area of expertise—nursing care.

These two trends affected the acceptability of a system of task allocation in two ways. First, because task allocation was associated

17

with non-individualised care, it became associated with *bad* care. Second, because task allocation was associated with assembly line working and bureaucratic organisation, it was seen as inimical to the professional approach to nursing.

Patient allocation on the other hand, was associated with both individualised care and the professional approach to nursing. At its simplest level patient allocation referred to a system of delivering nursing care where a nurse, or a group of nurses, was allocated to a patient, or a group of patients. However, regardless of variations in actual deployment patterns, the main difference between a system of patient allocation and a system of task allocation was that with patient allocation it was the patients and not the tasks which were allocated to the nursing staff on duty. In the nursing literature it was claimed that patient allocation was a better method of organising the delivery of nursing care than task allocation because it resulted in:

(i) improved patient care
(ii) greater job satisfaction for nurses

When this research study was being planned, there were two main problems which concerned the researcher. The first was that if a system of patient allocation was as advantageous as it was reputed to be, why, by 1978 was it not more widely practised?

The earliest reference found by the researcher, which documented the introduction of a system of patient allocation into the British nursing literature was in 1958 (Jenkinson, 1958). Yet Pembrey (1978) found that in her research study only 9 of 50 ward sisters used a method of organising the delivery of nursing care which could be described as 'patient allocation''.

The second problem which concerned the researcher was linked to the knowledge, seldom, if ever, officially documented, but known to "insiders" that in a number of instances where a system of patient allocation had been introduced, once the original instigator had left, the organisation of the delivery of care reverted back to the old task allocation system.

The most common explanation given for the lack of widespread use of patient allocation was a shortage of staff (Jenkinson, 1961; Miles, 1978). It was argued that since patient allocation required more staff, who were not available, then it could not be more widely implemented. However, many of the advocates of patient allocation claimed to have implemented it with *no* increase in staffing establishment (Auld, 1968; Pembrey, 1975; Chavasse, 1978). Explanations for the second problem mentioned above, have never been "officially" discussed, since the problem has never been "officially" recognised.

It seemed fruitful at this stage to take a broader view of the whole problem of why patient allocation was not more widely used, and examine it from the perspective of the hospital as an Organisation. Hospitals are large and complex organisations with an intricate network of formal and informal communications and social structure. The method of organising the delivery of nursing care is not a separate entity which can be examined in isolation for it is inextricably linked to the organisational and social structure of the hospital. Thus, in this study a more useful method of tackling the research problem appeared to be to introduce a system of patient allocation into one ward of a hospital and investigate the effects of the change upon the attitudes and activities of those involved—the nurses, the patients, and the other hospital staff.

However, a more detailed review of the literature highlighted yet another problem. Three experimental studies had previously been undertaken to test the reputed advantages of a system of patient allocation (Auld, 1968; Chavasse, 1978; Boekholdt and Kanters, 1978). But these three studies did not provide firm evidence to support the reputed advantages. All three studies found that although the nursing staff tended to like the new system, the patients noticed little difference. The usual explanation given for this lack of positive patient satisfaction was that the research instruments had been inadequate. Although this explanation may have been correct, a closer examination of the three studies revealed that there were methodological weaknesses in their experimental designs, which would call into question the findings which had been obtained (for a detailed critique of these three studies the reader is referred to the full report of the current research study (Metcalf, 1982).

Thus from the point of view of the current research study, two further research problems were raised:

—were the reputed advantages of a system of patient allocation really true? and
—why, despite a lack of reliable research evidence, was a system of patient allocation reputed to be so much better than a system of task allocation, any evidence to the contrary appearing to be conveniently ignored?

As a result, the research study developed from being solely an examination of a specific incidence of change to being in addition, an experimental study where a system of patient allocation was introduced into a ward of a hospital and the reputed advantages reassessed using a more rigorous experimental design.

1.3 Patient Allocation and the Nursing Process

The review of the literature quickly showed that there was considerable confusion surrounding the term 'patient allocation'. Because it was associated with 'professionalism' it obviously meant more than being simply a method of deploying nurses. Some people realised this, others did not. Some nursing sisters such as Mathews (1972) and Pembrey (1975) realised that to organise the delivery of care by allocating nurses to patients and not to tasks, other changes would have to be made; changes in ward organisation, changes in record keeping, changes in reporting, changes in accountability and responsibility. These were the changes that were linked to 'professionalism'. Other nursing sisters, however, did not realise this, and the researcher's own experience gained from working and visiting in several different hospitals, suggested that what passed for "patient allocation" was not uniform. A point which was also recognised by Moult et al. (1978) and Pembrey (1978). In some wards which claimed to use 'patient allocation' the nursing staff were given little information about the patients to whom they had been allocated, other than what 'tasks' needed to be carried out. Often they were not expected to write reports on their patients or contribute in any way to the planning of their care—these functions were still carried out by the ward sister or the nurse in charge. In other wards, however, the nursing staff were encouraged to write reports on their patients, attend and contribute in handover reporting sessions and liaise with medical and other hospital staff. On some wards the 'patient allocation' lasted until coffee break, after which it disintegrated. On other wards, nurses were allocated to the same patients for a few consecutive shifts.

The advent of the nursing process into the British nursing literature appeared to clarify the situation but in fact caused further confusion. The nursing process was described as a new philosophy of nursing based on a patient-centred approach to care (Norton, 1981). It emphasised assessing, planning, implementing and evaluating nursing care, according to the individual needs of the patient and it soon became 'officially adopted' by the then General Nursing Council for England and Wales. (GNC, 1977.) Patient allocation was then relegated to being a mere method of deploying nurses, albeit one which was consistent with the philosophy of the nursing process (Marks-Maren, 1978). Confusion arose because not all nurses appeared to realise this. Again, from the researchers own experience statements such as:

—"We're doing the nursing process" or
—"We're putting in the nursing process next week"

often meant little more than the fact that the ward sister was using a system of patient allocation (which still might break down after coffee break) and had acquired a larger "Kardex" on which could be recorded an increased number of 'personal details' about the patient. Thus the whole area was bedevilled by problems of nomenclature. When nurses and nursing sisters talked about the "nursing process" did they really mean "patient allocation"? But what did they mean when they talked about "patient allocation". Now in 1985 there is a considerable amount of information in the British nursing literature about the nursing process. When this study was planned, in 1978, there was much less, and what did exist was the subject of controversy. The work of Crow (1977) caused considerable scepticism among some nurses (Davis, 1977). More information about patient allocation was available but even so, the amount was still small. However, from reading both the literature on patient allocation and the nursing process it became apparent that the advantages to patients and staff which were reputed to result from using a system of patient allocation, were transferred "en bloc" to the nursing process (Marks-Maren, 1978).

1.4 The Present Study

The present study was carried out in a ward of a maternity hospital. The maternity area was chosen for a number of reasons, but one of the most important was expediency. The hospital was conveniently situated and the senior nursing staff and ward sisters were interested in the study. However, if the reputed advantages of a system of patient-centred care, either patient allocation, or the nursing process were true, then a maternity ward would be an excellent venue. Midwives are proud of their 'independent practitioner' status, and many of those who practise in hospitals are concerned that they are being reduced to the level of "maternity nurse" (Hockey, 1976). Those who are at the receiving end of maternity care (that is mothers themselves) are also concerned about the fragmentation of the hospital maternity service. Criticisms of lack of continuity, conflicting advice and impersonal treatment have figured prominently in the works of Kitzinger (1979), Cartwright (1979), Perkins (1978) and Oakley (1979). Dissatisfaction with the quality of the maternity services is also reflected in the establishment of groups such as the National Childbirth Trust (NCT) and the Association for the Improvement in Maternity Services (AIMS). Consequently, one could make an *a priori* assumption that any change which would make maternity care more "patient centred" would be welcomed by both mothers and midwives.

The confusion which surrounded both patient allocation and the nursing process caused problems for the present study. If the intention was to introduce and evaluate a system of patient centred care—what should it be; patient allocation or the nursing process? In the end the decision was made to introduce a system of patient allocation. This decision was based on three factors:

1. When this study was being planned, the nursing process was the subject of considerable controversy. It was felt by the then

Divisional Nursing Officer concerned, that the ward sisters might be willing to accept a system of patient allocation, but if the nursing process with all its emotional overtones was suggested, the study might never begin.

2. The nursing process is intended to be a more sophisticated approach to nursing care than is implied by a system of patient allocation. It involves assessing, planning, implementing and evaluating the care that a patient receives. If carried out in the manner in which it was intended, it necessitates considerable responsibility and autonomy to be delegated to nurses under the grade of ward sister. It was felt that it would be unrealistic to expect the nursing staff to be able to carry out these new roles without a considerable amount of prior training, and this could not be provided by the research funds or in the time available.

3. The care that a maternity patient receives in hospital does not begin in the hospital ward—it begins when she 'books in' at the ante-natal clinic, or perhaps even when she has her pregnancy confirmed by her general practitioner. The hospital ward, particularly the post-natal ward, is not the place to *start* taking nursing histories and making nursing assessments, although it may be the place to *continue* making them and updating them.

The system of patient centred care which was introduced in this study was a form of patient allocation. Its features are described in Chapter 3. Although it has some features in common with the nursing process, it was not intended to be a pseudonym for the nursing process. As argued above, the introduction of the nursing process into a maternity hospital should not start in a ward which was concerned with post-natal patients but in the ante-natal clinic or earlier. If the opportunity arose then the system of patient-centred care which was introduced by this study could be developed further at a later date.

CHAPTER 2

The Conceptual Framework and the Research Design

2.1 The Conceptual Framework

The conceptual framework for this study was based on the work of Hall, Pill and Clough (1976). They suggested that a hospital ward was like an arena where the various combinations of conflict and co-operation between social actors was played out. The assumptions behind the framework suggested by Hall, Pill and Clough, were that an individual's understanding of his/her situation would be derived from his/her past experience and his/her attitudes and values. However, they went on to suggest that evaluation of the present may react upon the definitions of the past and involve re-definition and reformation in the light of new events. They claimed that variables such as patient and nurse satisfaction can be examined within such a framework.

This framework suggested by Hall, Pill and Clough was considered by the researcher to be suitable for the present study. By considering interpersonal factors within a structural setting, it allowed the different perspectives of different individuals to be seen at all levels of participation in the ward. In addition, it also explicitly recognised that the attitudes, values and behaviour patterns that both mothers and nursing staff bring to the ward have an important affect upon the process of change, patient satisfaction and the job satisfaction of the nurses and midwives. Explanations for the effects of the change to a system of patient allocation could then be generated from the different perspectives.

Figure 1 is a diagrammatic representation of the conceptual framework used for the present study. It outlines and clarifies the main variables which are involved and illustrates the expected relationship between them, namely that:

(i) the attitudes, values and paradigms of care held by the nurses and midwives are assumed to affect patient care through the method used to organise the delivery of care. However, the method used to organise the delivery of care can itself influence the attitudes, values and paradigms of care of the nursing staff as can the nurses actual experience of giving care. These relationships are demonstrated in the work of Menzies (1960).

23

FIGURE 1
Diagram of the Basic Conceptual Framework for the Study

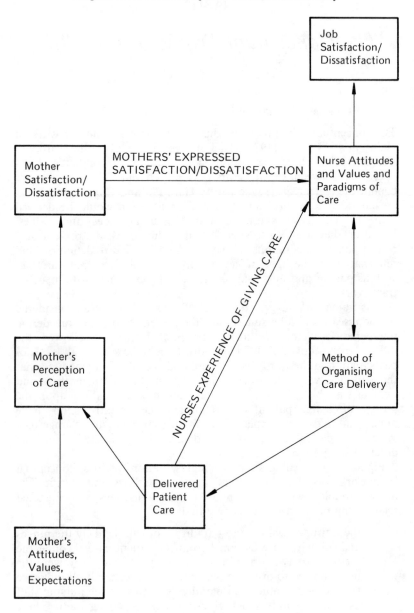

24

(ii) The mothers' perception of care is assumed to be influenced not only by the actual delivered patient care but also by the attitudes and values which the mother holds and with which she interprets and assesses delivered care. These attitudes and values can themselves be influenced by previous experience of receiving care.

(iii) The satisfaction or dissatisfaction of the mother with the care that she receives is assumed to depend upon her perception of that care. The mother's satisfaction or dissatisfaction with care (if it is expressed) is assumed to be an influence upon the attitudes, values and paradigms of care that the nurses and midwives hold.

(iv) The satisfaction or dissatisfaction of the nursing staff with their jobs is assumed to be a result of the degree to which their experience of giving care, their awareness of patient satisfaction or dissatisfaction with care, and their method of organising the delivery of care, are consistent with their own attitudes, values and paradigms of care.

If these assumed relationships are true, and if the method of organising the delivery of care is changed, one would expect to see changes in the various organisational variables occurring in the manner outlined above.

2.2 The Research Design

(a) *The 'Action' Approach*

The definition of the research as a study of a specific incidence of change necessitated a comparative and a descriptive approach. However, since another purpose of the research was to reassess certain hypothesised relationships between certain variables an experimental approach was also necessary. Furthermore, in order to make legitimate comparisons between the results of this study and those of other studies, it was necessary to ensure that the system of patient allocation which was introduced conformed, at least in general to certain specifications. In this particular study such an obligation meant that the researcher became involved in the implementation as well as the evaluation of the change. Thus it was necessary to adopt an 'action' research approach.

The 'action' approach to research, and its use in nursing research has been discussed by Clarke and Hockey (1979) and by Greenwood (1984). According to Clarke and Hockey (1979) one of the advantages of action research is that there is a better chance of change being implemented if and where appropriate. One of the disadvantages of action research is that generalisations cannot be made from the results—they are only applicable in the specific situation in which they

25

are studied. This does not mean that similar findings would not occur if the study were replicated elsewhere, but merely that they cannot be taken for granted. However, the scientific design of action research should be just as careful as that of other types of research, and all the normal principles relating to the research process should be applied.

Thus, to achieve the aims of the research study, the research design incorporated an 'experimental study' and an interview study. To facilitate the collection of data, the research was carried out in three distinct phases:

Phase I—the pre-change period.
Phase II—the change period.
Phase III—the post-change period.

(b) *The Periods of Data Collection*

Phase I—the pre-change period

The first phase of the research study was a descriptive analysis of the care given in the selected maternity ward. During this period, data about patient satisfaction with care and the job satisfaction of the nursing staff were collected. Additional data were collected by observing the nursing staff at work, with the intention of assessing any changes in nursing practice that resulted from the introduction of the system of patient allocation. Data of this type had not been collected in the previous similar studies, (Auld, 1968; Bockholdt and Kanters, 1978; Chavasse, 1978) but it would provide a useful background against which to interpret the data on patient satisfaction and staff job satisfaction.

Phase II—the change period

The second phase was the period of change when the staff on the 'research' ward changed their method of delivering nursing care to a system of patient allocation. During this period the researcher participated with the staff to help introduce the changes. Towards the end of this phase, interviews were used to assess the nursing staff's opinions about the changes. These data were supplemented by a 'diary of events' which was kept by the researcher during the period of change.

Phase III—the post-change period

The third phase of the research study was a descriptive analysis of the care given in the research ward after the system of patient allocation had been introduced. The data collected in this part of the study were similar to that collected in Phase I of the study. However, Phase III data were not collected until the system of patient allocation had been in operation for six months.

(c) *The 'Experimental' Study*

The data for the 'experimental study' were collected in phases I and III and were divided into three sections:

    (i) the observation study;
    (ii) the patient satisfaction study;
    (iii) the staff job satisfaction study.

The data collected were compared and subjected to a detailed analysis in order to determine if in fact the change to the system of patient allocation had made any difference to the variables being studied. A description of the data collected, and the instruments which were used for data collection is given in Chapters 5, 6 and 7 of this volume.

Experimental studies use the terms of independent and dependent variables. There is assumed to be a relationship between the independent variable and the dependent variable(s) so that manipulation of the independent variable would cause a change in the dependent variable(s). In this study, the method that the nursing staff used to organise the delivery of nursing care was considered to be the 'independent' variable. The 'dependent' variables were considered to be:

    (i) patient satisfaction with care;
    (ii) the job satisfaction of the nursing staff;
    (iii) observed work patterns.

The change in the 'independent' variable took place in phase II and the 'dependent' variables were measured in phases I and III; *before* and *after* the change in the independent variable.

(d) *Experimental Research, Design and Validity*

Although the validity of the design of any research study is always important, in experimental studies the validity of the design is crucial. Campbell and Stanley (1966) stated that there are two kinds of validity which are important in research design; internal validity and external validity. Internal validity asks the question:

"Did in fact the experimental treatments make a difference in this specific instance?"

External validity asks the question:

"To what populations, settings, treatment variables and measurement variables can this effect be generalised?"

27

Internal Validity

In experimental studies, in order to determine whether or not the experimental treatment did make a difference it is necessary to 'control' certain variables. Unfortunately, in some types of research settings for example nursing or teaching it is not always possible to control these variables. For example, in this study it was unlikely that the same mothers and nursing staff would be participating in both phases I and III of the research study. Such limitations do not necessarily mean that the research findings will be worthless, but they do make it more difficult to assess the actual effects of the 'independent' variable upon the dependent variables. Careful use of 'control' groups can in some cases help to minimise these problems and Campbell and Stanley (1966) referred to such research designs as *quasi-experimental*. In their book, Campbell and Stanley give eight different classes of extraneous variables relevant to internal validity which if not controlled for in the experimental and quasi-experimental design might produce effects which would be confounded with the experimental stimulus.

The internal validity of each of the three main areas of data collection in the 'experimental study' is considered in Chapters 5, 6 and 7. However, although individually each area of data collection in this study has limitations in the extent to which it can assess the effects of the experimental treatment, the number of different methods used, and the extent to which the findings of each are consistent with the findings of the others can be used to give support to various hypotheses. A technique described by Denzin (1970) as 'data triangulation'.

External Validity

In this study, because a case study approach is being used, the external validity is obviously limited. However, detailed small scale studies do have advantages (Perkins, 1980; Stacey and Homans, 1978). Such studies enable the research worker to examine the dynamics of a particular situation and the pressures that operate on staff to influence their behaviour. However, although many of these pressures can be caused by local or individual factors, Perkins (1980) argued that trying to explain good practice, or explain away bad practice in terms of the presence or absence of certain factors, does less than justice to those who manage well in difficult conditions. Perkins suggested that explanations based on individual or local characteristics are only partial and that the behaviour of, for example, personnel in maternity clinics, will not only be determined by their individual or local characteristics and local pressures, but also by the

". . . ordering of professional priorities which they have learned and which may have become instinctive" (Perkins, 1980, p. 17).

Because the external validity of this study is limited, there is no guarantee that the results of this study will be repeated elsewhere. This does not mean that they will not be, but merely that it cannot be taken for granted and each particular case will be a matter for empirical investigation.

(e) *The Interview Study*

The interview study was undertaken to ascertain if and/or how the changed method of organising the delivery of care made a difference to the nurses' and midwives' experience of giving that care. It was hoped that information about the process of change would be obtained and that some explanations for the lack of widespread use of a system of patient allocation could be suggested.

The permanent staff on the 'research' ward were interviewed along with the permanent staff on another ward in the hospital which had also decided to introduce a system of patient allocation but with which the researcher was not involved (see Chapter 4). The staff interviewed included sister midwives, staff midwives, nursery nurses and auxiliary nurses. Pupil midwives who had worked on the various wards in the hospital were also interviewed. Semi-structured interview schedules were used to guide the direction of the interviews but the nursing staff were all encouraged to speak freely about their experiences.

2.3 The Development of the Research Instruments and Pilot Studies

When using a longitudinal design, a pilot study in the customary sense of a "dress rehearsal" for the research study (Moser and Kalton, 1971) is impractical. A complete replication of the proposed study would have taken as long as the proposed study itself. However, it was still necessary to pre-test or pilot the proposed research instruments for the following reasons:

(i) to help guide the choice between alternative methods of data collection;
(ii) to ascertain the effectiveness of the research instruments, that is, do they gather the relevant data;
(iii) to discover and if possible resolve any practical problems relating to the use of the research instruments.

In this study the instruments used in each area of data collection were developed and piloted separately between January and April 1979. The development of the instruments used in each area of data collection are considered separately in Chapters 4, 5, 6 and 7.

2.4 Summary of the Research Design

Figure 2 is a diagrammatic representation of the research design showing the stages of the research and the main areas of data collection.

FIGURE 2
Diagram of Research Design and Areas of Data Collection

PRE-CHANGE		POST-CHANGE

Summer 1979		Summer 1980
1. Observation Study (research ward)	CHANGE	1. Observation Study (research ward)
2. Patient Satisfaction Study	PERIOD	2. Patient Satisfaction Study
(ante-natal clinic, research ward, post-natal clinic)	1. Interviews with research ward staff and pilot ward staff	(ante-natal clinic, research ward, post-natal clinic)
3. Nursing staff job satisfaction study		3. Nursing staff job satisfaction study
(research ward, control ward, pilot ward)	2. Diary of events	(research ward, control ward, pilot ward)

30

CHAPTER 3

The Changes and the Process of Change

3.1 Venue

The research study was carried out in a large urban maternity hospital. Initial negotiations for entry were made through the then Divisional Nursing Officer of the Maternity and Gynaecological Division. A research proposal was sent to the Division of Obstetrics and Gynaecology for approval and after this discussions took place with two sister midwives whom the Divisional Nursing Officer thought might be interested in the study. The sister midwives were willing to allow their ward to be used for the study provided that they had some guidance and support. It was pointed out to the sisters that the researcher was not in a position to *tell* the sisters what to do, but that ideas would be suggested and discussed. What was considered important was that for any changes to be successful, the sisters had to be happy with them and consider them feasible, for they, not the researcher were responsible for the day-to-day running of the ward.

3.2 A Description of the Research Ward in the Pre-change Period

(a) *The Ward*

The "research" ward, like all the other maternity wards in the hospital, admitted both ante- and post-natal patients, all, or at least most of whom were under the care of a single consultant obstetrician. The permanent staff on the ward included two sister midwives, one senior staff midwife, a nursery nurse, a nursing auxiliary, a ward clerk and a number of domestic staff. Part-time staff included two auxiliaries and a sister midwife. Junior staff midwives, pupil midwives and student nurses seconded from a nearby general hospital rotated through the ward as part of their training.

Figure 3 is a diagrammatic representation of the research ward. The ward was of a contemporary design with seven single rooms and four four-bed bays. The ward was structurally divided into two halves by the nurse's station. There were two large nursery rooms—one for each half of the ward. Meals were prepared and plated individually in the central kitchens and were distributed by the domestic staff.

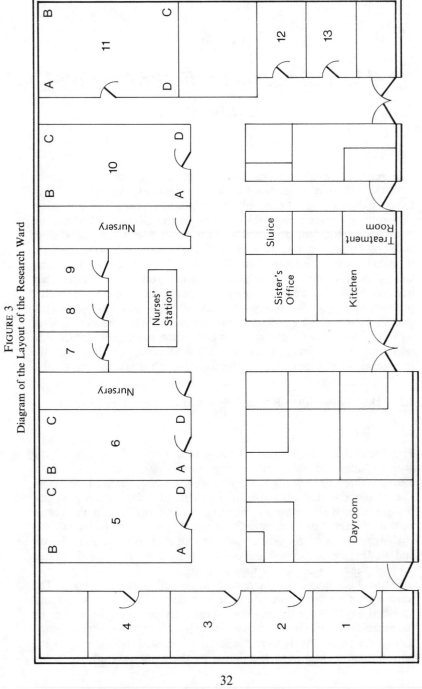

FIGURE 3
Diagram of the Layout of the Research Ward

Although the hospital was situated in a depressed inner city area, the fact that it contained many regional specialities meant that it also catered for mothers outside the immediate catchment area. Private patients were also accepted. Thus the social class composition of mothers was mixed.

In 1978, the usual length of stay in the ward was about four to five days for a mother with an uncomplicated first birth and about eight to ten days for mothers who had had caesarian sections or other complications. There was also an option of a 48 hour discharge for mothers whose deliveries had been uncomplicated and who had suitable home circumstances.

(b) *The Organisation and Allocation of Work*

The work of the nursing staff, both direct and indirect patient care, was organised according to the 'ward routine' which was displayed on the wall in the sister's office. The nursing staff on the ward adhered to the hospital policies of 'rooming-in' and 'demand feeding' but there were also other routines of patient care which, although they did not appear to be written down, were generally accepted and adhered to. For example, the time when a mother could have a shower/bath, the time when a mother could bath the baby by herself. The ward had two Kardex record holders, one for the ante- and post-natal patients and one for the babies. No prescriptions for care were written in the Kardex, it was simply a record of the patients' and the babies' conditions. The Kardex was written twice daily.

The sister and all the morning staff received a report from the night nurse at 7.45 am. The report was descriptive, not prescriptive. The night nurse gave a report on each patient's physical and emotional condition and mentioned any changes which had occurred during the previous night. The day nurses often added remarks about a particular patient's emotional condition, however, guidance was seldom given about how or by whom a particular patient should be approached. After the morning report, the nurses and midwives on duty were allocated to either the 'ward' (where they looked after the mothers) or the 'nursery' (where they looked after all the babies). The daily workload for the ward was organised using three main work books; the 'treatment' book, the 'mothers' book, and the 'baby' book. After the report the sister or midwife in charge visited each patient with the specific intention of "seeing how they all are and sorting out any problems". She usually made these visits alone.

Although the nursing staff were allocated to specific areas, the system was flexible and if the balance of work between the 'ward' and the 'nursery' altered so that one area became busier than the other then staff from the other area would help out. In both the 'ward' and the 'nursery' the staff organised among themselves who would do what work. However, it did appear that certain staff had 'established rights' to certain jobs. Certain jobs in the ward were performed by particular grades of staff because of their position in the hierarchy. Other jobs were performed by particular staff members by custom and these customs varied between the wards of the hospital.

The staff on the afternoon shift came on duty at 12.45 pm and received a report from the sister or midwife in charge. Since the 'nursery' work was usually finished by lunchtime, no specific allocation of the available staff to any area of the ward was made. After the report, the morning staff all went to lunch and the afternoon staff commenced the daily observation of temperature, pulse, blood pressure etc. and these were usually finished by the time the morning staff returned from lunch. Any specific tasks which needed to be carried out during the remainder of the shift were usually allocated on an *ad hoc* basis.

Liaison with the medical staff was conducted mainly through the ward sister. During the main weekly ward round the consultant was accompanied by the ward sister or the midwife in charge. If possible, a pupil midwife would also be present. On other mornings, when the Senior House Officer and the Registrar saw the patients they might, or might not, be accompanied by a member of the nursing staff. If the nursing staff were busy the medical staff did not insist on their presence, but liaised with them before and after the ward round. When a member of the paediatric house staff came to the ward, he or she was usually taken round the babies by the nursery nurse (who appeared to have 'established rights' to this job).

(c) *Standards of Care*

It is difficult to make objective comments about standards of care when nationally agreed acceptable standards do not exist. The dissatisfaction of some mothers and midwives with the present organisation of hospital maternity care has been discussed elsewhere and a number of problems have been highlighted (Metcalf, 1982; Hale, 1985). This research study was undertaken from the standpoint that similar dissatisfactions *could* exist in this hospital but no attempt was made to demonstrate this.

In fact, the care given to patients in the research hospital was classed by Kitzinger (1979) in the 'Good Birth Guide' as "exceptionally good". Kitzinger's classification system was based on recommendations from 1,759 women who had replied to her request for information about British maternity hospitals. The hospitals which were considered to be 'exceptionally good' were places where: ". . . freedom of choice and respect for the individual is linked with human caring; where one's partner is given a warm welcome, there is opportunity for full discussion concerning medical procedures, support for coping in labour whatever way one wishes and where it is accepted that the baby belongs to the parents and is not the property of the hospital" (Kitzinger, 1979, p. 19).

Although the research hospital was reputed to be one of the best of those surveyed by Kitzinger, this does not mean that no mother or midwife was, or never could be, dissatisfied with the care given in that hospital. However, the fact that the hospital was generally considered to be "good" and to have a flexible approach to patient care, may have accounted for the willingness of the senior nursing staff and the ward staff to allow the researcher access to the hospital.

3.3 The Changes Which Were Introduced

(a) *The Principles Underlying the Changes*

One of the aims of the research project was to introduce a system of patient centred care into the research ward. However, from the previous description of the pre-change organisation of the delivery of care, it is apparent that although patient care may have been *task-centred* it was seldom *task-allocated*. The nursing staff exercised a certain amount of flexibility when organising their work and the mothers were not subjected to rigid routines. Although some routine did exist it appeared to the researcher, who had spent a considerable period of time observing the mothers and the nursing staff, that the organisation of the delivery of care had over the years been modified to take account of changes in hospital policies such as the introduction of 'demand feeding' and 'rooming in'. However, although these new policies had led to modifications in what previously would have been a more rigid approach to care, the basic structure of the organisation of the delivery of care had not changed and by 1978 it was to some extent anachronistic. In a ward which encouraged 'rooming-in' and 'demand feeding' the division into 'ward' and 'nursery' was artificial, for in reality these divisions no longer existed. The allocation of the nursing staff to either the 'ward' or the 'nursery', meant that the care of the mother and her baby was fragmented. One nurse or midwife looked after the mother and her problems, while another looked after the baby and his/her problems. No-one cared for the mother and baby together and dealt with their joint problems (except perhaps the nursery nurse who appeared to have 'established rights' over the supervision of breast feeding).

The primary aim of the system of patient centred care which was to be introduced into the ward was to enable the nursing staff to care for, or learn to care for the mother and baby as a 'unit' without being hindered by outdated functional divisions. The system of patient allocation which was to be introduced was not ideal—but it was what suited the ward at that time and one with which the nursing staff on the research ward felt they could cope. The changes which were to be introduced were grouped into three main areas:

1. the allocation of work;
2. the planning and recording system;
3. associated practices.

(b) *The Changes in the Allocation of Work*

Because of the differentiation of staff and the type of ward design, it was decided, at least initially, to divide the mothers into two groups, consistent with the design of the ward. One group of mothers would be those in beds 1–7, the other group would be those in beds 8–13. (See Figure 2.) Each group of nurses and midwives would be caring for mothers in both single rooms and four-bed bays and each 'patient group' would contain a mix of ante-natal mothers, post-natal mothers and babies. Each nursing team would contain a mix of the staff on duty (that is, midwives, pupil midwives, student nurses, auxiliaries and nursery nurses) with the most senior midwife in each team being considered the team leader. (In practice, each team rarely consisted of more than two staff members, one of whom would usually be an auxiliary or a nursery nurse with the other being a staff midwife, pupil midwife, or occasionally a student nurse.)

Each morning, after the 7.45 am report, the nursing staff on duty were to be divided into the two teams and allocated to a group of mothers and babies. The staff coming on duty at 12.45 pm would also be allocated to one of the two groups of mothers and until 4.15 pm would work with the morning staff who had cared for those mothers during the morning shift.

(c) *Changes in the Planning and Recording System*

The work books were to be discontinued and replaced by developing the Kardex system. The two Kardex would still be used but now one was allocated to each group of mothers—a baby's file being placed immediately after his or her mother's file. The Kardex system was improved so that there was space to write a brief plan of care for each person. These plans were to be written daily by the team leader.

(d) *Changes in Associated Practices*

Continuity of care was to be the aim, so it was hoped that, as far as possible, staff would be allocated to the same group of mothers and babies for more than one shift. Team leaders were encouraged to liaise with the medical and other hospital staff about the patients in their care. After the early morning report, each team would visit each person in their care and discuss with her the plan of care for that morning. Team leaders were encouraged to give the lunch-time report of their own patients—with all the morning shift staff present.

3.4 Associated Events

Immediately prior to the introduction of the changes on the research ward, three events took place which indirectly affected the introduction of the changes. One of these events was the scheduled visit from the Inspectors of the then Central Midwives Board. The Inspectors stressed the 'advantages' of using a patient centred approach to care and noted with regret the presence of task centred methods of record keeping such as the ward work books. This visit stimulated an interest in patient centred care in one of the other ward sisters. She decided that she too would like to introduce a system of patient allocation. Although the researcher was not specifically involved with this ward, the network of informal communications in the hospital ensured that the two systems were similar and because of this it was possible to obtain some valuable data from the staff on this ward. Data from this ward (called the 'pilot' ward in the study) were used in the interview study and the job satisfaction study.

A second event was a meeting between the research ward nursing staff and the ward medical staff (obstetric and paediatric) which took place in October, 1979. The purpose of this meeting was to discuss the proposed changes with the medical staff and obtain their co-operation. Generally the changes were favourable received. The opportunity was also taken to discuss some of the patient care routines (particularly the unwritten ones!). It transpired that the Consultant was as unaware of the origins of many of them as were the nursing staff. It was decided to introduce more flexibility into patient care and 'routines' of care were to be considered as guidelines with the nursing staff allowed considerable discretion in interpreting them. Thus this meeting, apart from generating general goodwill between the nursing and medical staff, also gave the nursing staff a certain amount of flexibility in the interpretation of what had often previously been considered as inviolable rules of patient care.

The third event which took place immediately prior to the introduction of the "changes" in the research ward was some change in the senior nursing staff of the research ward. At the end of August, 1979, the senior sister left to take up a post overseas. Her place was taken by the previous junior sister who had recently returned from maternity leave and a new junior sister was appointed. The senior staff midwife was pregnant and left in November, 1979. Thus the beginning of the change to a system of patient allocation coincided with a marked change in senior midwives and although all the new staff members were in favour of the system of patient allocation it did mean that the effects of a change in senior staff could become inextricably entwined with the effects of change to a system of patient allocation. Similar changes in senior nursing staff did not occur on the other ward where a system of patient allocation was introduced but with which the researcher had no direct involvement.

3.5 The Time Scale of the Changes

The changes in patient care were introduced, not overnight, but gradually over a few weeks with some changes following on logically from others. For example, the removal of the work books was closely followed by the new method of allocating staff. The staff, now working in their new 'teams' quickly realised that the system of having one Kardex record holder for the babies and one for the ante-natal and post-natal mothers, was no longer suitable—both teams always wanted the same Kardex at the same time. Consequently, each team was given a Kardex record holder for its own patients. Following this, the changes in the 'associated practices' began to be introduced. First it was decided that each nursing team would visit each of the mothers in their group after the early morning report and that all the morning staff would be present at the lunch time report. Shortly after this, each team was made responsible for writing their own Kardex reports and for giving the lunch time report on their own patients. It is also important to emphasise that once a 'change' had been introduced it did not always mean that care was always delivered in that fashion. There were occasions when the nursing staff reverted to their old practices and these were usually occasions of some temporary crisis, for example, heavy workload or reduced staff. However, as the staff gained familiarity and confidence with the new methods of working, then gradually the 'reversions' became less frequent.

CHAPTER 4

The Interview Study

4.1 Introduction

The data presented in this chapter form a background to the data collected in the experimental study which is described in Chapters 5, 6 and 7. The main purpose of the interview study was to ascertain if the changed method of organising the delivery of care affected the nurses and midwives experience of giving that care and if so, how. Using the method of 'data triangulation' described in Chapter 2 the data described in this chapter were used to support, or not support, the findings of the other areas of data collection.

In April, 1980, shortly before the post-change observation study commenced, the permanent staff on the 'research' ward (excluding the ward sisters) were interviewed. The staff on the 'pilot' ward were interviewed as a check on the validity of the responses of the staff on the 'research' ward. The pupil midwives and ward sisters were not interviewed until October 1980. Altogether a total of 20 people were interviewed. All the interviews took place in the respective wards, while the staff were on duty. The most suitable time was either late morning, or in the afternoon. A semi-structured interview schedule was used to guide the direction of the interviews but the nursing staff were encouraged to speak freely about their experiences. Although the interview schedules varied slightly in layout and detail, they were all designed with the following aims:

(i) To obtain the nurses and midwives interpretation of the changes which had taken place.

(ii) To obtain the nurses and midwives perception of how their work had changed.

(iii) To obtain the nurses and midwives perception of how specific aspects of their work had or had not changed. These aspects were:

   (a) relationships with colleagues;
   (b) contact with patients.

(iv) To explore what the nurses and midwives meant by a system of patient allocation and whether they thought they were carrying out the system.

(v) To ascertain what the nurses and midwives considered to be the disadvantages and the advantages of a system of patient allocation, and the main obstacles to organising work in that way.

(vi) To explore what the nurses and midwives meant by the term 'individualised care' and whether they thought they were giving more 'individualised care' than before.

Unfortunately in this volume lack of space precludes a detailed discussion of the responses of the various staff members to the interviews. Outlined below is a selection of what the researcher considered to be the most salient points raised by the interviews. These were:

Changes in the work roles of the various members of the ward staff. The opinion of the nursing staff about the advantages and disadvantages and obstacles to a system of patient allocation. The meanings that the nurses and midwives attached to 'individualised care'.

4.2 Changes in the Work Roles of the Various Members of the Nursing Staff

The majority of the staff interviewed on both the 'research' ward and the 'pilot' ward said that they liked the system of patient allocation. However, it appeared that the extent to which the actual work roles of the staff were affected was not uniform. Those members of staff whose work roles appeared to be most affected by the changes were the auxiliaries, the nursery nurses and the junior pupil midwives. Those less affected appeared to be staff midwives, the senior pupil midwives and the ward sisters.

Both the increase in information which resulted from the changed method of organising the delivery of care, and the new organisational arrangements themselves were appreciated by the auxiliary nurses who felt that they could envisage their workload more easily and could remember the various problems of particular patients. As a result of this, they felt that their relationship with the patients had improved. Such effects are consistent with the reputed advantages of a system of patient allocation which were discussed in Chapter 1. However, not all members of staff found their work roles enhanced. The nursery nurse on the research ward felt that her work role had been diminished because she had lost some of the autonomy and responsibility that she had previously acquired. As explained above, the nursery nurse on the 'research' ward had 'established rights' to the supervision of breast feeding mothers—and she was very good at her job. She considered the mothers who were breastfeeding to be 'her group' and in effect she resented having to share these mothers with a member of staff from the other 'team'. However, the experience of the nursery nurse on the 'pilot' ward suggests that the pre-change work role of the nursery nurse on the 'research' ward may not have been typical of all nursery nurses employed in hospital maternity wards. The nursery nurse on the 'pilot' ward was very much in favour of the new system. She felt that her job had been made more interesting because now she did not spend most of her time in the nursery bathing babies but could help with the mothers generally. She felt that she was now able to look after the mother and baby together instead of always having to look after the babies alone.

The more 'senior' the nursing staff on both the 'research' ward and the 'pilot' ward, the less they appeared to feel that their actual work role had changed, although most approved of the changed organisational arrangements. The more 'senior' the staff on the ward, the more likely they were to be left in charge of the ward and, therefore, the more information they were likely to be given regardless of the system used for organising the delivery of care.

The work role of the ward sister appeared to change less than the reputed advantages of a system of patient allocation would suggest (Matthews, 1972; Pembrey, 1975). To some extent this was possibly a result of the organisational position of the ward sister within the hospital. A sister's organisational position is at the boundary of the ward and the larger hospital system (Pembrey, 1978). More than any other position in the ward, her work role is influenced by the expectations of those external to the ward. Thus one of the sisters on the 'research' ward said that even when she allocated herself to a group of patients, she kept having to return to her office to deal with various problems. Doubtless some of the interruptions could have been prevented by foresight and improved organisation, and in time possibly would have been. However, many interruptions occurred because other hospital personnel and some visitors wished to see sister, and only sister.

All the sisters were agreed that the system of patient allocation was better for the education and training of the pupil midwives because they were given more responsibility, to which after initial help, they usually adapted well. One of the pupil midwives felt that the new system gave them more opportunity to initiate discussions with the mothers about various aspects of health such as contraception.

The part-time ward sister, who worked mainly on the evening shift, found that her work role was affected by the system of patient allocation which was introduced. She usually came on duty at about 4.30 pm to be 'in charge'. With the abolition of the 'work books' she found that it took her longer to become acquainted with the immediate workload of the ward and this, quite understandably, disturbed her.

This problem experienced by the part-time sister further highlights the inter-relationship between the various facets of the hospital organisation. The system of 'work books' with its emphasis on 'tasks' was consistent with the hierarchical organisation of the hospital because it made senior staff interchangeable in the short term. Although the full time ward sisters had a long term responsibility for their wards, being 'in charge' on a particular shift meant little more than making certain that the necessary work was carried out competently. By introducing a system of delivering nursing care which recognised patient care as being more than a series of tasks, and by altering the planning and recording system so that successful delivery of care depended on some measure of continuity of staff, difficulties were created for a member of staff who came in two or three evenings a week to be "in charge". The role of the part-time workers within a system of patient allocation will be discussed in the final chapter.

4.3 The Opinions of the Nursing Staff about the Advantages and Disadvantages and Obstacles in a System of Patient Allocation

(a) *Advantages*

For most of the staff members the advantages of a system of patient allocation centred around:

  (i) knowing more about the patients;
 (ii) being able to spend more time with patients and follow-up problems; this was felt to be advantageous for both patients and nurses;
(iii) less stress on 'getting the work done';
 (iv) an improved learning situation for the pupil midwives because they obtained some experience in organising care for a group of patients and were also able to care for the mother and baby as a 'unit'.

(b) *Disadvantages*

Not all the staff interviewed felt that there were disadvantages and some felt that the advantages out-weighed the disadvantages. However, the disadvantages that were mentioned are outlined below:

  (i) a nursery nurse and a junior staff midwife said that their lack of knowledge about the patients and babies to whom they were *not* allocated meant that if a doctor or visitor requested information about these patients, they had to go and find someone who did know. Having to do this they said, made them feel rather stupid.
 (ii) the possibility of personality clashes between a patient and a nurse was mentioned by a senior staff midwife and one of the auxiliaries; however, in practice, no problem of this nature had been experienced.

(iii) the problem of an 'unreliable' nurse was raised by a junior staff midwife who felt that it would be difficult to trust such a nurse and give her responsibility if she had made mistakes in the past.

(c) *Obstacles*

The problem of staff shortages were mentioned by all the staff. This included both the quality (that is the number of qualified staff) and quantity (that is the number of staff) on duty. The auxiliaries felt that because of the limitations of their role they needed to have a nurse or midwife working with them, otherwise someone had to come from the other teams to attend to the patients' observations and this detracted from the ideals of patient allocation. A junior staff midwife felt that the attitude of the staff to a system of patient allocation was as important as staff numbers.

4.4 The Meanings that the Nurses and Midwives Attached to 'Individualised Care'

For the staff, definitions of individualised care centred around:

  (i) care planned to suit specific needs of specific patients;
  (ii) one nurse caring for the total needs of the patient;
 (iii) treating the mother and baby as a unit;
 (iv) treating the mothers and babies as individuals with specific problems;
  (v) following up problems;
 (vi) making the patient feel that she is special and she is not just being treated the same way as everyone else.

All the nursing staff except the nursery nurse on the 'research' ward felt that they gave the patients more 'individualised care' than before. However, they did not think that they were noticeably more 'flexible' than before. According to one of the auxiliaries the 'ward routine' had initially become more flexible when 'demand feeding' had been introduced. As far as she was concerned, the system of patient allocation had meant that the staff were less concerned about keeping to a strict time schedule, but the consensus of opinion was that they had always been quite 'flexible'.

The nursery nurse did not feel that she gave more 'individualised care' than before. As far as she was concerned the system of patient allocation gave the nurses and midwives the opportunity to get to know 'their' patients better, but how they then treated them depended on the personality and training of the particular nurse or midwife.

CHAPTER 5

The Observation Study

5.1 Summary of Data Collected

The following data were collected and examined during the observation study:

(a) The work that the nursing staff actually did was observed and recorded. This was done by:

(i) observing and recording how certain members of the nursing staff spent their time on particular shifts. In the pre-change period seven members of staff were observed for two shifts each, morning shift and afternoon/evening shift. In the post-change period eight staff members were observed again for two shifts each. All grades of staff were represented and all the observed staff worked on the research ward;

(ii) observing the care given to certain patients. Twelve mothers on the 'research' ward were observed in both the pre- and post-change periods. Again the morning and afternoon periods were covered.

(b) The periods of interaction between the nursing staff and patients were observed to show:

(i) the length of each period of interaction;
(ii) the number of different patients with whom each staff member interacted;
(iii) the number of staff interacting with one particular patient;
(iv) the initiating factor in the interactions;
(v) who initiated the interaction.

To facilitate the collection of these data, the periods of data collection in the observation study were organised into two parts; the nursing staff observation study and the patient observation study. The research methods of non-participant observation and continuous observation were used.

Data for the observation study were collected on the 'research' ward in phase I before the changes in the method of organising the delivery of care were introduced, and again in phase III after the changes had been introduced. Although all the patients and a number of the staff observed were different in the two periods of data collection, the first period of data collection acted as a control for the second period and any differences in the variables measured were noted.

5.2 The Validity of the Design of the Observation Studies

The main problem in designing the 'experimental' study was trying to separate effects which could be due to the manipulation of the independent variable (in this case the method of delivering care) from the effects of other variables such as:

the 'Hawthorne' effect;
different ward sisters;
different staff being observed;
different patients being observed.

Because so many of these other variables could not be controlled in this research study, the design of the observation study was limited in that (as must always be remembered) any changes in the observed variables may not have been due solely to the change in the method of delivering care; and the research findings must be interpreted in the full knowledge of this limitation.

5.3 The Development of the Research Instruments and Pilot Studies

The activities and interactions which were relevant to the present study were pre-coded and categorised to facilitate analysis. Recording schedules were specially designed so that the data could be punched directly from the recording sheet on to the computer card. An example of the recording sheet can be seen in Appendix A.

The code lists which were eventually used to categorise nursing and patient activities and nurse patient interaction were mainly developed during informal periods of observation on the maternity ward. The nursing activity code list was supplemented by coding categories used by other researchers for example Moult *et al.* (1978), and Auld (1976).

(a) *Nursing Staff Observation Study Codes*

(i) *coding of nursing activities*
For the purposes of this study, the activities of the nursing staff were divided into seven sections:

basic	—0	communication	—4
technical general	—1	administration	—5
technical midwifery	—2	unclassified	—6
education	—3		

Each section was sub-divided into activities. An example of the code list and the activities included in a category is given in Appendix B.

45

(ii) *coding of the initiating factors in the nurse-patient interaction*

During the period of informal observation on the ward, the reason for every nurse patient interaction was recorded. At the end of the informal periods the initiating factors were grouped into categories and coded. A copy of the code list which was finally compiled can be found in Appendix C.

(iii) *identification of mothers*

In the nursing staff observation study the interactions between one nurse and all the patients were observed. The mothers were identified by bed number so that every interaction of the nurse could be linked to a specific mother.

(b) *Patient Observation Study Codes* (only post-natal patients were included in these observations).

(i) *coding of the nurse-patient interactions*

In the patient observation study, the interactions between the mothers and the nursing staff were observed to record with whom each mother interacted, for how long, who initiated the interaction and what was the initiating factor in each interaction. The same initiating factor codes as described above were used. Each nurse was given a code number by grade. A copy of the nurse grade codes and the patient observation study recording sheet can be seen in Appendix D and E.

(c) *The Pilot Study*

The pilot study was composed of four observation sessions, two for nurses and two for patients. When observing the nursing staff, the researcher started observing at the beginning of the nurse's shift, either 7.45 am or 12.45 pm and continued observing until the end of that shift, either 4.15 pm or 9.15 pm. Breaks were taken with the nurse. During the patient observation study the mother was observed from either 8.00 am to 3.00 pm or from 4.00 pm to 9.15 pm. During the morning observation session a short break of about 15 minutes was taken around 12.45 pm when the number of nurses on the ward was minimal. During the evening observations a break was taken between 7.30 pm and 8.30 pm when visitors were present. No observations were made between 3.00 pm and 4.00 pm, again because visitors were usually present and there was rarely any nurse-patient interaction during this period.

All activities and interactions were timed using a digital card watch attached to the researcher's clip board. It was felt that stop watch precision was unnecessary but times were recorded to their nearest second. Activities were not broken down into their component parts and thus activity codes were broad. Occasionally the researcher had to make an arbitrary decision about the start and finish of certain activities. If any uncoded activities occurred during the pilot study, they were allocated a code number.

Apart from some minor modifications to the code list the method of data collection proved to be satisfactory. A list of rules for observation was drawn up for use in the main study to ensure consistency between the periods of data collection. A copy can be found in Appendix F. By remaining at some distance but within earshot, the researcher was able to observe and follow both nurses and mothers without disturbing them unduly. If there was any doubt about what a nurse was doing, if for example she was behind a screen, then the researcher asked the nurse for an explanation of her activity.

5.4 The Main Study

(a) *Selection of the Sample*

The nurses and midwives who were observed during the study were chosen from those working on the "research" ward when data collection commenced. Since it was assumed in this study that each individual nurse or midwife observed would be representative of all nurses and midwives in that grade, matched pairs of nurses and midwives were obtained for the pre- and post-change periods. For this reason, no nurse or midwife who was new to the ward was observed. Those members of the nursing staff who were not permanent staff members had all been working on the ward for more than two weeks before they were observed. The nursery nurse and the nursing auxiliary were observed in both the pre- and post-change periods.

Because of the constraints on time and the wish to cover most of the weekly period, it was not possible to select a matched sample of mothers for the pre- and post-change observation sessions. The mothers were observed on their second, third or fourth post-natal day and were selected solely according to the length of time they had been on the ward. During the afternoon/evening before a planned observation session a particular mother who met the selection criteria was asked by the researcher if she would be willing to participate in the study. Only one mother declined to participate. The choice of 'suitable' mothers was sometimes limited because some mothers were being discharged 48 hours after delivery.

(b) *Hours of Observation*

In phase I the observed members of staff consisted of:

one sister midwife;	one student nurse;
one staff midwife;	one nursery nurse;
two pupil midwives (one senior (A));	one nursing auxiliary.
(one junior (B));	

Each member of staff was observed for two shifts each; the morning shift 7.45 am–4.15 pm (shift 1) and the afternoon shift 12.45 pm–9.15 pm (shift 2). An exception was made for the nursing auxiliary who on shift 1 was only observed from 7.45 am–1.00 pm. Thus in phase I the total number of hours observed was 116.

When the observation study was repeated in phase III similar observations were made on the same grades of staff. However, in phase III both sister midwives were observed for two shifts each. Both sisters were observed in the post-change period because their particular methods of managing the system of patient allocation differed slightly and it was considered useful to include both in the observation study. In the pre-change period, because the system of managing the ward work had been long established both sisters had similar management styles. In phase III the nursing staff were observed for a total of 133 hours.

The observation periods were arranged so that as far as possible the weekly period was covered. This meant that induction days, clinic days and admitting days would all be included in the data collection period, thereby covering busy as well as quiet periods.

In the patient observation study, in both phases I and III, 12 post-natal mothers were observed continuously from either 8.00 am–3.00 pm (shift 1) or 4.00 pm–9.15 pm (shift 2). The weekly period was again covered except that Sundays were excluded from the observation periods. The mothers were observed for a total of $73\frac{1}{2}$ hours in both the pre- and post-change periods.

(c) *Analysis of Data*

The results obtained from the data collected in the pre- and post-change periods were compared using a number of statistical tests. In the nursing staff observation the test most frequently used for comparison was the Wilcoxon Matched Pairs Signed Rank Test. The data obtained from each grade of nurse or midwife observed in the pre-change period were compared with that obtained from the same grade of nurse or midwife observed in the post-change period. The test was complicated by the fact that in the post-change period two sisters were observed. Rather than take an average of the results of both sisters to use as a basis for comparison, it was decided that it would be more exact to use the results obtained from both sisters and perform the tests twice. In the nursing staff observation study the lengths of the observation periods varied slightly because a particular nurse might still be working on the ward after her shift had officially finished. In view of this, it was decided to compare the percentages of time that the observed staff members spent on their various activities and in interactions.

In the patient observation study, the data obtained from the

48

observations on each shift in the pre- and post-change periods were compared and tested for significant differences, using in most instances the Mann and Whitney U Test. Because each mother was observed for the same length of time the comparisons between the pre- and post-change data were made using the actual times of the activities and interactions.

For both the Wilcoxon Matched Pairs Signed Rank Test and the Mann and Whitney U test a significance level of 5% or less was considered to be indicative of a possible change. However, it must be remembered that in cases where the sample sizes are small (as in this study) then:

(i) it is unlikely that any highly significant results will be obtained from using the statistical procedures;

(ii) any significant results which do appear should be treated with caution because they may not actually indicate genuine population differences.

In these cases the value of using statistical procedures is that it is an objective method of ordering the data and the results of the tests can be used to indicate *trends* in the data. What becomes important then is not so much the actual level of significance of the results of any one test, but the manner in which the results fit together and how changes in one area are reflected by corresponding changes in another area.

(d) *The Nursing Staff Observation Study*

The main findings are presented under the following headings:

(i) the activities of the observed members of the nursing staff;
(ii) the interactions between the nursing staff and the mothers;
(iii) the length of time of the nurse-patient interactions;
(iv) the initiating factors in the nurse patient interactions.

(i) *The activities of the observed members of the nursing staff*
In the study the activities of the observed members of the nursing staff had been coded and grouped into seven categories:

basic nursing	—0	communication	—4
technical nursing (general)	—1	administration	—5
		miscellaneous	—6
technical nursing (midwifery)	—2		
education	—3		

Table 1 shows the percentage of observed time spent by the observed members of the nursing staff in each of the above categories in shift 1 of the pre- and post-change periods. The percentage of total observed time that each individual spent in each activity category in

LIBRARY
SOUTH LOTHIAN COLLEGE OF NURSING & MIDWIFERY
ROYAL INFIRMARY, LAURISTON PL., EDINBURGH

TABLE 1
The Percentage of their Total Observed Time that Each Observed Staff Member Spent
in Each Activity Category

N = Total Observed Time (in minutes)

ACTIVITY CATEGORIES

	Staff	0	1	2	3	4	5	6	N
	Sister	3%	14%	17%		37%	8%	21%	502·99
	Staff Midwife	13%	8%	7%	7%	21%	19%	26%	484·91
(a) Shift 1 pre-change	Pupil Midwife (A)	22%	13%	2%		22%	6%	35%	498·29
	Pupil Midwife (B)	17%	16%	12%	1%	20%	13%	20%	483·4
	Student Nurse	25%	6%	8%	5%	19%	6%	31%	501·94
	Nursery Nurse	28%		18%		23%	5%	25%	490·65
	Auxiliary	35%		15%		24%		26%	327·87

	0	1	2	3	4	5	6
Results of Wilcoxon Matched Pairs Signed Rank Test Between Each Activity Category	NS @ 5% level	NS @ 5% level	NS @ 5% level	NS @ 5% level	Sig* @ 5% level	NS @ 5% level	NS @ 5% level

* $0·05 > p > 0·02$.
NS = Not significantly different

	Staff	0	1	2	3	4	5	6	N
	Sister (A)†	8%	20%	7%	1%	43%	5%	16%	509·64
	Sister (B)	4%	11%	4%		60%	3%	17%	513·42
	Staff Midwife	10%	7%	10%	4%	40%	9%	20%	510·05
(b) Shift 1 post-change	Pupil Midwife (A)	6%	21%	14%	6%	21%	3%	29%	509·52
	Pupil Midwife (B)	18%	26%	6%	1%	25%	7%	16%	502·17
	Student Nurse	18%	21%		4%	26%	7%	24%	509·63
	Nursery Nurse	14%		2%	3%	41%	1%	38%	511·0
	Auxiliary	17%		15%	3%	31%	3%	31%	510·0

† The tests were performed twice so that the data from each Sister could be used. The significance levels refer to *both* tests.

the pre- and post-change periods was compared and tested by shift, using the Wilcoxon Matched Pairs Signed Rank Test. The results of the test suggested that in shift 1 of the post-change period there was a significant increase $(0.05 > p > 0.02)$ in the percentage of time spent in activities falling into the category "communication".

A breakdown and analysis of the activities which constituted the category "communication" suggested that the increase in shift 1 of the post-change period had been caused by the individual members of staff spending a greater percentage of their time in "ward report" and on "medical ward rounds". It had not been caused by an increased percentage of time being spent interacting with the patients. This increased percentage of time spent in the activities of "ward report" and "medical ward rounds" is not in itself unexpected. Because of the changes in practice which were introduced with the system of patient allocation, all or at least most, of the nursing staff on duty attended the lunchtime report, and this change by itself would increase the total amount of time that observed staff members spent in the activity of "ward report". However, Table 2 indicates that after the change to the system of patient allocation, the early morning ward report for the staff on shift 1 tended to be longer. In the pre-change period, the

TABLE 2

The Length of Time that Each Individual Observed Staff Member Spent in the 7.45 am Ward Report on Shifts 1 of the Pre- and Post-change Period

	Length of Ward Report (in minutes)		Length of Ward Report (in minutes)
Sister	10·57 m	Sister (A)	14·50 m
Staff Midwife	8·42 m	Sister (B)	7·98 m
Pupil Midwife (A)	13.10 m	Staff Midwife	22·33 m
Pupil Midwife (B)	13·92 m	Pupil Midwife (A)	14·82 m
Student Nurse	7·42 m	Pupil Midwife (B)	5·97 m
Nursery Nurse	10·42 m	Student Nurse	12·80 m
Nursing Auxiliary	10·31 m	Nursery Nurse	12·20 m
		Nursing Auxiliary	24·92 m

(a) Shift 1—Pre-change

(b) Shift 1—Post-change

51

TABLE 3

The Percentage of their Total Observed Time that Each Observed Staff Member Spent
Interacting with Patients

(N = total observed time in minutes)

		%	N		%	N
	Sister	40%	(502·99)	Sister (A)	27%	(509·64)
	Staff Midwife	21%	(484·91)	Sister (B)	24%	(513·42)
	Pupil Midwife (A)	36%	(498·29)	Staff Midwife	29%	(510·05)
(a) Shift 1	Pupil Midwife (B)	47%	(483·4)	Pupil Midwife (A)	44%	(509·52)
	Student Nurse	26%	(501·94)	Pupil Midwife (B)	41%	(502·17)
				Student Nurse	43%	(509·63)
	Nursery Nurse	23%	(490·65)	Nursery Nurse	13%	(511·00)
	Auxiliary	45%	(321·87)	Auxiliary	34%	(510·00)

(i) Pre-change

(ii) Post-change

Results (a)—Not significant at 5% level using data from both Sisters in post-change
period—(Wilcoxon Matched Pairs Signed Rank Test)

		%	N		%	N
	Sister	30%	(501·06)	Sister (A)	29%	(513·02)
	Staff Midwife	29%	(491·42)	Sister (B)	41%	(503·65)
	Pupil Midwife (A)	40%	(497·19)	Staff Midwife	29%	(508·6)
(b) Shift 2	Pupil Midwife (B)	46%	(523·27)	Pupil Midwife (A)	54%	(509·96)
	Student Nurse	26%	(513·29)	Pupil Midwife (B)	41%	(511·27)
				Student Nurse	22%	(509·06)
	Nursery Nurse	34%	(533·6)	Nursery Nurse	29%	(513·06)
	Auxiliary	26%	(481·92)	Auxiliary	42%	(314·93)

(i) Pre-change

(ii) Post-change

Results (b)—Not significant at 5% level using data from both Sisters in post-change
period—(Wilcoxon Matched Pairs Signed Rank Test)

average length of the ward report was 10·58 minutes, in the post-change period it was 14·44 minutes. This increase in the length of time was caused by the sister or midwife in charge being more specific about prescribing patient care to the morning staff after the night nurse had finished her report.

There were no significant differences in the percentage of time spent in activities falling into the other six main activity categories, neither were there any significant differences when the data obtained in shift 2 of the pre- and post-change periods were compared and tested.

(ii) *The interactions between the nursing staff and the mothers*
Table 3(a) and (b) show the percentage of observed time and actual times (in minutes) that the observed members of the nursing staff spent interacting with the mothers in shifts 1 and 2 of the pre- and post-change period. The percentages were compared and tested using the Wilcoxon Matched Pairs Signed Rank Test but the results of the test suggested that there were no significant differences in the percentages of time that the nursing staff spent interacting with the mothers between the pre- and post-change periods.

(iii) *The lengths of the nurse patient interactions*
The actual lengths of all nurse patient interactions for the whole sample of observed nursing staff were calculated and grouped into the following categories:

(a) short under $2\frac{1}{2}$ minutes;
(b) medium $2\frac{1}{2}$ minutes and over—less than 5 minutes;
(c) long 5 minutes and more.

Table 4 shows the number of interactions falling into each category. The data were compared using the Chi-Squared Test. On shift 2 the proportions falling into each category in the post-change period were significantly different from the proportions falling into the same categories in the pre-change period. $(0·05 > P > 0·02)$. An

TABLE 4
The Number of Nurse-Patient Interactions Falling into the 'Short', 'Medium' and 'Long' Categories for Each Shift in the Pre- and Post-change Periods

	Shift 1		Shift 2	
	Pre-change	Post-change	Pre-change	Post-change
(a) short	305	312	368	354
(b) medium	78	79	70	107
(c) long	53	70	60	69

N.S. at 5% level $0·05 > p > 0·02$
(Chi-Squared Test)

53

TABLE 5

The Percentage of Nurse-initiated Interactions which Fell into Each Initiating Factor Category for Each Observed Staff Member on Shifts 1

	A	C	D	E	G	H	I	J	K
Sister	45%	25%	8%	17%	2%	2%	—	2%	—
Staff Midwife	63%	8%	10%	—	2%	—	2%	2%	13%
Pupil Midwife (A)	47%	10%	10%	3%	19%	—	—	4%	8%
Pupil Midwife (B)	42%	23%	7%	15%	5%	—	1%	5%	—
Student Nurse	49%	17%	11%	4%	2%	—	8%	8%	—
Nursery Nurse	17%	31%	22%	11%	5%	3%	5%	3%	3%
Auxiliary	27%	19%	11%	—	8%	—	8%	—	27%

(a) Shift 1 pre-change

	A	C	D	E	G	H	I	J	K
Sister (A)	71%	22%	5%*	—	—	2%	—	2%	—
Sister (B)	28%	55%	9%	4%	1%	—	—	1%	1%
Staff Midwife	60%	26%	7%	—	5%	—	—	—	2%
Pupil Midwife (A)	68%	17%	6%	2%	2%	2%	—	—	2%
Pupil Midwife (B)	62%	20%	8%	—	—	—	2%	—	8%
Student Nurse	57%	3%	3%	—	6%	1%	1%	—	29%
Nursery Nurse	—	18%	4%	18%	21%	—	7%	11%	21%
Auxiliary	44%	13%	8%	3%	5%	—	8%	8%	13%

(b) Shift 1 post-change

Results of Wilcoxon Matched Pairs Signed Rank Test for percentage falling into each category	NS @ 5% level	NS @ 5% level	Sig* @ 5% level	NS @ 5% level	NS @ 5% level	unsuitable data		NS @ 5% level	NS @ 5% level

* $0.05 > p > 0.02$. The Wilcoxon Matched Pairs Signed Rank Test only recorded a significant difference when the data from Sister (A) were used in the test. When the data from Sister (B) were substituted and the test repeated the difference was not significant at the 5% level. The data in categories H & I was unsuitable for the Wilcoxon Matched Pairs Signed Rank Test.

TABLE 6

The Percentage of Nurse Initiated Interactions which Fell into Each Initiating Factor
Category for Each Observed Staff Member on Shifts 2

		A	C	D	E	G	H	I	J	K
	Sister	31%	44%	3%	3%	9%	—	—	8%	—
	Staff Midwife	78%	13%	6%	—	—	—	—	3%	—
(a) Shift 2 pre-change	Pupil Midwife (A)	49%	12%	3%	2%	27%	—	—	7%	—
	Pupil Midwife (B)	67%	9%	8%	2%	6%	—	1%	3%	4%
	Student Nurse	54%	22%	1%	—	4%	—	8%	7%	1%
	Nursery Nurse	34%	31%	5%	12%	2%	—	9%	7%	—
	Auxiliary	28%	8%	12%	—	4%	—	16%	16%	16%

		A	C	D	E	G	H	I	J	K
	Sister (A)	59%	21%	6%	6%	1%	—	3%	4%	—
	Sister (B)	63%	13%	10%	3%	5%	2%	—	3%	—
	Staff Midwife	72%	18%	11%	—	1%	—	—	5%	—
(b) Shift 2 post-change	Pupil Midwife (A)	72%	9%	2%	4%	4%	—	4%	6%	—
	Pupil Midwife (B)	66%	19%	5%	1%	1%	—	—	4%	3%
	Student Nurse	58%	21%	—	3%	5%	—	—	5%	8%
	Nursery Nurse	29%	33%	—	18%	7%	—	4%	9%	—
	Auxiliary	38%	—	1%	3%	3%	—	3%	13%	3%

Results of Wilcoxon Matched Pairs Signed Rank Test for percentages falling into each category	NS @ 5% level	NS @ 5% level	NS @ 5% level	NS @ 5% level	NS @ 5% level	unsuitable data		NS @ 5% level	unsuitable data

The results refer to tests where the data from both Sisters in the post-change period
were used. The data in categories H and I were unsuitable for the Wilcoxon Matched
Pairs Signed Rank Test.

examination of the data suggested that there was a marked increase in the proportion of interactions falling into the medium range, that is lasting $2\frac{1}{2}$ minutes or over, but less than 5 minutes. There was no significant difference in the proportions falling into each category in shifts 1 of the pre- and post-change period.

(iv) *The initiating factors in the nurse-patient interactions*
The initiating factor categories described above were used to give some indication of the nature of the interactions between the nursing staff and the mothers. Since the majority of interactions were 'nurse' initiated then it is the initiating factors in these interactions which are discussed below.

Table 5(a) and (b) and Table 6(a) and (b) show the percentage of nurse initiated interactions falling into each initiating factor category. The code list for the initiating factors can be found in the Appendix C. The low percentage of initiating factors falling into the categories of "education" (E) and "emotional support" (H) do not necessarily

TABLE 7

Total Nurse-Patient Interaction Times (in minutes) for Each Observed Mother

(Mothers identified by code number)

	Mother	Pre-change	Post-change	Mother
(a) Shift 1	101	47·57 m	112·92 m	203
	103	52·53 m	69·98 m	204
	106	34·12 m	51·02 m	206
	108	42·88 m	70·65 m	207
	110	69·42 m	26·28 m	209
	111	48·28 m	44·20 m	212
	Total	294·8 m	375·05 m	

Results of Mann & Whitney U Test (a) differences not significant at 5% level

	Mother	Pre-change	Post-change	Mother
(b) Shift 2	102	9·45 m	15·65 m	201
	104	17·62 m	26·97 m	202
	105	8·73 m	23·53 m	205
	107	14·58 m	39·77 m	208
	109	16·78 m	10·92 m	210
	112	25·02 m	13·38 m	211
	Total	92·18 m	130·22 m	

Results of Mann & Whitney U Test (b) differences not significant at 5% level.

reflect the actual percentage of interactions which were concerned with these activities. In some cases although the interaction may have developed into an educational or counselling session, the initial (apparent) reason for the interaction was different. Thus the recording of the apparent initiating factor between the nurse and the mother can give only a crude measure of the nature of the interactions which took place.

The percentage of interactions falling into each category was compared by shift using the Wilcoxon Match Pairs Signed Rank Test. In some cases there was insufficient data to carry out the test. In shift 1 (Table 5(a) and (b)) when the data from sister midwife A were used in the calculations the results it was suggested that there was a significant decrease $(0·05 > p > 0·02)$ in the percentage of interactions initiated by category "D" that is the observed staff member giving or asking the mother for information. However, when the data from sister midwife B were substituted and used in the calculation the difference was not significant. There were no significant differences between any of the other categories in shift 1 and between any of the categories in shift 2.

(e) *The Patient Observation Study*

The main findings are presented under the following headings:

(i) the interactions between the observed mothers and the nursing staff;
(ii) the lengths of time of the nurse-patient interactions;
(iii) the initiating factors in the interactions between the patients and the nursing staff.

(i) *The interactions between the observed mothers and the nursing staff*
The total amount of time that each individual mother spent interacting with members of the nursing staff was calculated for shifts 1 and 2 of the pre- and post-change period. The data obtained are displayed in Table 7(a) and (b). The data obtained were compared by shift using the Mann and Whitney U Test. The results of this test suggested that there were no significant differences between the pre- and post-change periods in the amount of time that individual mothers spent interacting with members of the nursing staff.

Table 8(a) and (b) shows the total *number* of interactions which occurred between the observed mothers and members of the nursing staff in each shift of the pre- and post-change periods. The data were compared using the Mann and Whitney U Test and the results suggested that the number of nurse patient interactions in shift 1 of the post-change period was significantly greater $(0·05 > p > 0·02)$ than the number occurring in shift 1 of the pre-change period. There was no significant difference in the number of interactions occurring in shifts 2 of the pre- and post-change periods.

57

TABLE 8

Total Number of Nurse-Patient Interactions for Each Observed Mother

(Mothers identified by code number)

	Mother	Pre-change	Post-change	Mother
(a) Shift 1	101	20	23	212
	103	12	14	209
	106	19	21	207
	108	16	23	206
	110	18	23	204
	111	17	25	203
	Total	102	129	

Results of Mann & Whitney U Test (a) differences significant at 5% level $0.05 > p > 0.02$

	Mother	Pre-change	Post-change	Mother
(b) Shift 2	102	7	8	211
	104	7	13	210
	105	6	8	208
	107	11	11	205
	109	10	7	202
	112	8	10	201
	Total	49	57	

Results of Mann & Whitney U Test (b) differences not significant at 5% level.

(ii) *The lengths of time of the nurse-patient interactions*
The lengths of all the interactions between the nursing staff and the observed mothers were grouped into the three categories:

(a) short—under $2\frac{1}{2}$ minutes
(b) medium—$2\frac{1}{2}$ minutes or over—under 5 minutes
(c) long—5 minutes or over

The data falling into each category are displayed in Table 9. The data were compared using the Chi Squared Test but there were no significant differences in the proportion of interactions falling into the three categories in either shifts 1 or 2 of the pre- and post-change period. Thus, the increased number of nurse-patient interactions which occurred on shift 1 of the post-change period occurred in the same proportion as before that is a large number of brief interactions, but few long ones.

(iii) *The initiating factors in the nurse-patient interaction*
The initiating factor of each interaction between a member of the

TABLE 9
The Number of Interactions by Shift Falling into the 'Short', 'Medium' and 'Long' Categories in the Pre- and Post-change Periods

	Shift 1		Shift 2	
	Pre-change	Post-change	Pre-change	Post-change
(a) Short	63	78	39	42
(b) Medium	26	27	6	5
(c) Long	13	24	4	10

N.S. at 5% level   N.S. at 5% level
(Chi-Squared Test)

nursing staff and the observed mothers was noted using the same categories as were used in the nursing staff observation study. Since most of the interactions were initiated by the nursing staff then only the initiating factors of the nurse initiated interaction are considered here.

Tables 10(a) and (b) and 11(a) and (b) show the percentages of all nurse initiated interactions falling into each of the relevant initiating factor categories described in Appendix C. The data falling into each category were tested using the Mann and Whitney U Test. The data in some categories were insufficient for testing.

On shift 1 (Table 10(a) and (b)) the results of the test suggested that there was a significant increase $(p = 0.002)$ in the percentage of interactions falling into category 'C' (surveillance). Thus the increased number of nurse initiated interactions which occurred in shift 1 of the post-change period (Table 8) was probably due to an increase in the number of "surveillance" interactions.

On shift 2 (Table 11(a) and (b)) the results of the Mann and Whitney U Test suggested that there was a significant increase $(p = 0.002)$ in the percentage of interactions falling into the initiating factor category A (clinical). The results also suggested that there was a significant decrease $(p = 0.02)$ in the percentage of interactions falling into category D (information).

Thus in shift 2 in the post-change period, there had been mainly a redistribution in the types of initiating factor in the nurse initiated interactions, with more interactions between nurse and mother being initiated by 'clinical' activities and less by the nurse either giving the mother information or asking the mother for information.

(d) *Summary of Results*

The findings of the observation studies suggested that there were in fact very few significant differences in the observed parameters of

59

TABLE 10

The Percentages of Nurse-initiated Interactions for Each Observed Mother which Fell
into Each Initiating Factor Category on Shift 1

(Mothers identified by code number)

	Mother	A	C	D	E	G	I	J	K
(a)	101	67%	7%	0%	13%	13%	—	—	0%
Shift 1	103	56%	0%	22%	11%	—	—	—	11%
pre-change	106	35%	12%	29%	—	—	6%	—	18%
	108	40%	7%	27%	—	7%	—	—	20%
	110	21%	7%	28%	7%	—	21%	—	14%
	111	63%	6%	6%	6%	—	—	—	19%

Results of Mann & Whitney U Test	NS at 5% level	Sig* at 0·2% level	NS at 5% level	insufficient data	NS at 5% level

* p = 0·002
NS = difference not significant

	Mother	A	C	D	E	G	I	J	K
(b)	212	42%	17%	9%	4%	9%	—	—	23%
Shift 1	209	32%	27%	9%	5%	5%	—	5%	18%
post-change	207	45%	36%	5%	—	—	—	—	14%
	206	35%	18%	6%	6%	18%	—	6%	29%
	204	36%	18%	9%	—	—	—	—	18%
	203	33%	22%	17%	6%	—	6%	—	17%

nursing staff activity and nurse patient interaction between the pre-
and post-change periods. The majority of the significant differences
that there were tended to occur on shift 1 although there were some
significant differences occurring on shift 2.

The possibility was considered that the differences which were
obtained were due to inconsistent coding on the part of the
researcher, especially since the time period between the pre- and post-
change observation periods was approximately one year. However,
given that the "rules for observation" had been established in the pre-
change period and were carried out by the researcher at every
observation session in both pre- and post-change periods, the
possibility of coding errors is reduced. Moreover, the inconsistency of
the significant differences between the pre- and post-change periods
make it less likely that the differences were being caused by
inconsistent coding. The question of whether the changes which did
occur were in fact due to the system of patient allocation which was
introduced will be considered in Chapter 8.

TABLE 11

The Percentages of Nurse-initiated Interactions for Each Observed Mother which Fell
into Each Initiating Factor Category on Shifts 2

(Mother identified by code number)

	Mother	A	C	D	E	G	H	I	J	K
(a)	102	0%	50%	17%	—	17%	—	—	17%	0%
Shift 2	104	0%	40%	0%	20%	—	—	—	20%	20%
pre-change	105	0%	0%	20%	20%	—	—	—	20%	20%
	107	22%	44%	11%	11%	—	—	20%	0%	0%
	109	0%	11%	33%	—	—	22%	11%	22%	11%
	112	14%	42%	14%	14%	—	—	—	0%	14%

	A	C	D		G	H			
Results of Mann & Whitney U Test	Sig* at 0·2% level	NS at 5% level	Sig* at 2% level	insufficient data	NS at 5% level	NS at 5% level			

* p = 0·002   * p = 0·02.
NS = difference not significant

	Mother	A	C	D	E	G	H	I	J	K
(b)	201	40%	30%	0%	—	10%	—	—	10%	10%
Shift 2	202	29%	14%	0%	—	14%	—	—	14%	29%
post-change	205	56%	11%	0%	—	—	—	—	0%	33%
	208	86%	14%	0%	—	—	—	—	0%	0%
	210	36%	27%	9%	—	—	—	—	9%	18%
	211	50%	0%	0%	—	12%	—	—	12%	25%

CHAPTER 6

The Patient Satisfaction Study

6.1 Summary of the Data Collected

In both the pre- and post-change periods, the patient satisfaction study consisted of three periods of data collection:

(i) a sample of mothers attending the ante-natal clinic completed an "expectation questionnaire";

(ii) a proportion of the above group were interviewed in hospital on the "research" ward shortly after they had had their babies;

(iii) a proportion of the group interviewed in hospital were re-interviewed in the post-natal clinic six weeks after discharge.

The first period of data collection acted as a 'control' for the second, and any differences in the variables examined were noted. The pre- and post-change samples consisted of different individuals.

6.2 The Validity of the Research Design of the Patient Satisfaction Study

As with the observation studies, the validity of the research design of the patient satisfaction study was limited because of the number of intervening variables which could not be controlled and which could have affected both the expectation of the mothers and the satisfaction of the mothers with the care they received. An example of a variable which could not be controlled was the fact that the groups of mothers whose expectations and satisfaction were assessed in the pre- and post-change periods were composed of different individuals. In addition, the members of the nursing staff with whom each group had contact during their pregnancy were also different in the pre- and post-change periods. Consequently, any changes which did occur between the pre- and post-change periods may not have been due solely to the change in the method of delivering care and the research findings must be interpreted in the full knowledge of this limitation.

6.3 The Development of the Research Instruments and Pilot Studies

(a) *The Assessment of Expectations*

The expectations of the mothers were assessed by administering a structured questionnaire to a sample of mothers who were attending the ante-natal clinic of the consultant obstetrician whose patients normally received their post-natal care on the 'research' ward.

The main aim of the 'expectation' questionnaire was to provide the researcher with a base from which the actual experiences of the mothers could be assessed. It was constructed following the steps outlined by McKennel (1974).

(i) The "universe of content" was explored empirically using unstructured interviews.
(ii) The content of the interviews was analysed.
(iii) An item pool was made up and the questionnaire developed.
(iv) The questionnaire was tested through a pilot study.

A copy of the 'expectation' questionnaire used in the main study can be found in Appendix G. The questionnaire consisted of 13 questions, the first 12 of which consisted of six pairs of 'polar opposites'. The 'polar opposite' questions were used as a method of checking the reliability of the questionnaire. The precise details of the development of the questionnaire can be found in the main study (Metcalf, 1982).

(b) *The In-patient Interviews*

The in-patient interviews had three main aims:

(i) To assess how far the expectations of the mothers had been met.
(ii) To provide the researcher with a data base of 'care received' and satisfaction with 'care received' which would provide a basis for comparison between the pre- and post-change periods.
(iii) To elicit:

(a) the opinions of the mothers in the pre-change sample about the 'idea' of a system of patient allocation;
(b) the opinions of the mothers in the post-change sample about their experience of a system of patient allocation.

Thus part of the interview was based on the areas covered in the 'expectation' questionnaire, part was concerned with care received and satisfaction with care received in specific areas, and part was concerned with the system of patient allocation.

The specific areas of care about which patient satisfaction was assessed were those concerned with the psycho-social aspects of care, since those were the areas which were reputed to be improved by a system of patient allocation.

(c) *The Post-natal Interviews*

The main purpose of the post-natal interview was to ascertain if, after six weeks at home, the mothers had changed their view of their hospital stay.

Copies of the interview schedules used in the in-patient interview study and the post-natal interview study can be found in the thesis (Metcalf, 1982).

The mothers in the study tended to refer to all members of the ward nursing staff as "the nurses" thus in the questionnaires and interview schedules the title "nurse" refers to any member of the ward nursing staff.

6.4 The Main Study

(a) *Selection of the Sample*

In both the pre- and post-change periods the samples of mothers were obtained by listing all the women whose expected delivery dates (EDDs) fell between two specified dates in the June and July of 1979 and 1980 respectively. Women who were in-patients at the time the list was compiled, as well as those who became in-patients before the questionnaire could be administered, were excluded from the sample. Asian women were also deleted from the list because they often had a poor command of English and this would have made it difficult for them to complete the questionnaire unaided. All the mothers in both samples were under the care of one particular consultant obstetrician; the one whose patients were normally admitted to the ward on which the system of patient allocation was introduced that is the "research" ward.

(b) *The Data Collection Periods*

(i) *The expectation questionnaire*

In both the pre- and post-change periods the mothers in the sample were contacted and the questionnaire administered when the researcher attended the ante-natal clinic of the consultant obstetrician. The appointment book had been checked in advance so that the researcher knew which mothers would be attending the clinic on that particular day. The study was explained to the mothers, confidentiality was assured, and they were all given the opportunity to refuse to participate. Those who agreed to participate were given a copy of the questionnaire which they then completed themselves. The researcher was available to help them with problems if they arose and all completed questionnaires were collected before the mothers left the clinic. In the pre-change period, at the end of three clinic sessions, 38 questionnaires had been completed. Forty mothers had been approached; one declined to participate and another misunderstood the instructions. This latter questionnaire was discarded. In the post-change period, at the end of three sessions, 41 questionnaires had been completed, and no one had declined to participate.

(ii) *The in-patient interviews*
In the pre-change period 25 mothers were interviewed. In the post-change period 33 mothers were interviewed. The attrition of the original sample was caused mainly by some mothers receiving their post-natal care on other wards in the hospital because no beds had been available in the 'research' ward at the time of their admission. Most of the mothers were interviewed shortly before their discharge, however, on two occasions, one in the pre-change period and one in the post-change period, the mothers were leaving for home just as the researcher arrived on the ward. Both these mothers invited the researcher to complete the interview in their own homes a few days later.

(iii) *The post-natal follow up interviews*
In both the pre- and post-change periods 15 mothers were interviewed when they attended the post-natal clinic six weeks after discharge. Some of the mothers interviewed in hospital had not wished to attend the hospital clinic for their post-natal check, while others failed to keep the appointment.

(c) *Analysis of Data*

The data obtained in the pre- and post-change period were compared and where possible and appropriate, subjected to statistical analysis. In this part of the study the test most frequently used was the Chi-Squared Test. In some cases, however, there was insufficient data to perform the test. Only a selection of the total data analysis is presented here.

(d) *The Expectation Questionnaire*

All the mothers who completed the 'expectation' questionnaire were asked to supply the following details:

How many children do you have?
Did you have any in this hospital?
Have you been in hospital before? (Apart from having babies.)
Have you been going to

(a) parentcraft or mothercraft?
(b) relaxation classes?

Have you been visited at home by the midwife?
Have you been shown

(a) the room where you will have the baby?
(b) the ward where you will be after you have had the baby?

It was considered that these variables might have some effect upon the expectations of the mothers. Table 12 shows the distribution of

TABLE 12
Comparison of Sample Variables for the Pre- and Post-change Expectation
Study

Sample Variables	Pre-change	Post-change
Women expecting first child	17	17
Women with other children	21	24
Women who had had a previous confinement at this hospital	14	17
Women who had been in hospital for reasons other than childbirth	13	25
Women who had been attending parentcraft/mothercraft classes	12	6
Women who had been attending relaxation classes	19	16
Women who had been visited at home by the midwife	15	17
Women who had seen the labour rooms	8	4
Women who had visited the post-natal wards	11	5
	N = 38	N = 41

sample variables between the two groups of mothers. The Chi-Squared Test was applied to the pre- and post-change data displayed in Table 12. There was only one difference significant at the 5% level between the two samples and that was in the number of mothers who had previous experience of hospitalisation other than pregnancy. In the pre-change period it was 13. In the post-change period it was 25 ($p = 0.02$).

The results of the pre- and post-change expectation questionnaires
For each of the first 12 questions in the expectation questionnaire the respondents had a choice of five answers:

definitely yes; quite likely; don't know; unlikely; definitely no.

In question 13 the respondents had a choice of three answers:

yes; don't know; no.

A summary of the pre- and post-change responses to this questionnaire is given in Table 13. For the purposes of comparison, the numbers falling into categories 'definitely yes' and 'quite likely' and categories 'definitely no' and 'unlikely' were combined for each

TABLE 13
Summary of Responses to the Pre- and Post-change Expectation Questionnaires

		Definitely Yes	Quite Likely	Don't Know	Unlikely	Definitely No
Question 1	Pre	32	6	—	—	—
	Post	29	10	1	1	—
Question 2	Pre	—	1	3	23	11
	Post	—	2	2	23	14
Question 3	Pre	12	17	3	4	2
	Post	13	13	5	9	1
Question 4	Pre	1	10	2	8	17
	Post	2	2	6	9	22
Question 5	Pre	—	10	6	15	6
	Post	1	9	8	16	7
Question 6	Pre	32	6	—	—	—
	Post	32	8	1	—	—
Question 7	Pre	12	12	8	5	1
	Post	15	13	9	3	1
Question 8	Pre	16	19	2	—	1
	Post	14	22	2	3	—
Question 9	Pre	13	12	4	6	3
	Post	11	15	5	2	8
Question 10	Pre	10	14	8	6	—
	Post	8	21	5	7	—
Question 11	Pre	2	5	2	23	6
	Post	—	3	3	26	9
Question 12	Pre	—	1	1	19	17
	Post	—	2	2	13	24

		Yes	Don't Know/ Uncertain	No
Question 13	Pre	18	11	9
	Post	22	11	8

question and the pre- and post-change responses compared using the Chi-Squared Test. Only in question 4 ('I expect that I will only be able to have my baby with me when he/she needs to be fed, changed or bathed') was there any difference significant at the 5% level between the pre- and post-change responses. In the post-change period less mothers expected the above, and more were unsure of what to expect. There were no significant differences between the pre- and post-change responses to any of the other questions.

The reasons the mothers gave for expecting to enjoy or not to enjoy their stay in hospital (question 13)

In both the pre- and post-change periods, most of the mothers who were expecting their stay in hospital to be enjoyable wrote that it was because they had had an enjoyable experience previously. Some mothers mentioned that it was because of the experienced staff who would be looking after them, while others wrote that they were looking forward to the 'rest'!

The reasons that the mothers gave for *not* expecting their stay to be enjoyable were mainly that they had had a difficult experience on a previous occasion and that they were expecting the birth to be painful and uncomfortable. In the pre-change period, one mother wrote that she had a general dislike of hospitals while in the post-change period, two mothers wrote that they would miss their homes and their husbands. Most of the mothers who were uncertain of what to expect were about to have their first child.

(e) *The In-patient Interviews*

For the purpose of comparison between the samples of mothers interviewed in the pre- and post-change periods, the following information was collected about each mother:

age; type of delivery; chosen feeding method; smoking habits; day on which interviewed; type of room; socio economic class.

In terms of these sample variables there were no differences significant at the 5% level (Chi-Squared Test) between the mothers interviewed in the pre- and post-change periods.

(i) *How far were the mothers expectations met?*

For the purposes of analysis the 12 expectation statements which formed the six pairs of polar opposites were combined and rephrased into the six 'expectation statements' described below:

expectation 1
The mother expected that the nurses in the hospital would teach her how to bath and feed her baby, and that they would not be too busy to do this.

expectation 2
The mother expected that if she had any problems she would be able to ask the nurses for help and that they would not be too busy to deal with them.

expectation 3
The mother expected that she would be able to feed her baby whenever she thought he/she was hungry, and not at set times.

expectation 4

The mother expected that she would be able to have her baby with her all the time and not just when the baby needed to be fed, changed or bathed.

expectation 5
The mother expected that the nurses would come round and ask her if she was having any problems and that they would not be too busy to do this.

expectation 6
The mother expected that in the ward, after she had had her baby, she would be looked after by a lot of different nurses and not just by one or two.

The results of this section of the interview analysis suggested that the majority of mothers in both the pre- and post-change periods had 'high' expectations about the care that they would receive in hospital and the majority found that their expectations were satisfied. In most cases, those few mothers who had had low expectations found that they were pleasantly surprised. There were only a few instances where 'high' expectations had not been realised, or 'low' expectations had been realised. In some cases this had been caused by unforseen circumstances, for example a caesarian section.

The experience of the mothers in response to expectation 6 merited further examination.

Table 14 shows the number of mothers in the pre- and post-change periods who said they were looked after by:

(i) a lot of different nurses
(ii) a lot of different nurses but familiar faces kept coming back
(iii) just a few nurses.

TABLE 14
Number of Interviewed Mothers who Received the Different Types of Nursing Attention in the Pre- and Post-change Periods

Nursing attention	Mothers Pre-change	Mothers Post-change
'lots of nurses'	21	15
'lot—but some familiar faces'	3	10
'just a few'	1	8

The numbers falling into the different categories were compared using the Chi-Squared Test. The differences were significant at the 1% level ($\chi^2 = 9.2$ 2D.F., $p = 0.009$). The significance of this observation lies in the mothers experience of the system of patient allocation in operation. The findings of the observation study suggested that some changes had occurred, albeit small, but they did not indicate if the changes were reflected in changes in the patients' experience. The length of the post-partum stay in hospital for the majority of mothers is very short, approximately 2 to 4 days. Given the shift system that the nurses work, then it is quite possible for a mother to claim that she "never saw the same nurse twice" during her stay. The figures displayed in Table 14 suggest that in the post-change period the mothers were more likely to see the same nurse twice even though there was very little difference in the actual quantity of nurse patient contact as measured in the observation study.

(ii) *"Care received" and satisfaction with "care received"*
The comparison of the pre- and post-change responses to this section of the analysis of the interview data suggested that there was little difference in the satisfaction of the mothers with the care that they received in hospital. In both the pre- and post-change periods the majority of mothers were very satisfied. The results also suggested that in both the pre- and post-change periods the mothers received similar care. Of particular interest in this section were the responses to the question: "while you have been in hospital do you feel that the nurses have treated you as an individual, or do you feel that you have been treated as just another mother with just another baby?"

In the pre-change period, 14 mothers said that they felt they had been treated as 'individuals' five felt that they had not been, and six were unsure. In the post-change period 25 mothers felt that they had been treated as individuals, two felt that they had not been and six were unsure. Although there was an increase in the number of mothers who felt that they had been treated as an 'individual' in the post-change period the differences were not significant at the 5% level.

The various reasons that the mothers gave for feeling that they were treated as 'individuals' were grouped into categories. The categories, together with the number of mothers who gave reasons which fell into that category are shown below: some mothers gave more than one reason.

Reasons why mothers felt they were treated as individuals	No. of mothers who gave the reason	
	pre-change	post-change
(1) having problems or worries taken care of adequately, that is not being 'fobbed off'	6	2

(2) nurses being flexible with the ward routine	1	3
(3) nurses knowing about 'your' problems and following them up	1	6
(4) nurses spending time with you	4	6
(5) nurses calling you by 'your' own name (that is not 'Mother')	5	11
(6) nurses chatting to you about 'your' home life/children/work	2	5
(7) the friendliness and helpfulness of the nurses	2	4
(8) continuity of nurses/seeing familiar faces	—	4

(iii) *The opinions of the mothers about the system of patient allocation*

The Pre-change Period

In the pre-change period the 'idea' of a system of patient allocation was explained to the mothers and they were asked for their opinions:

Thirteen mothers liked the 'idea';
Five mothers did not like the 'idea';
Seven mothers were ambivalent and did not think that it would matter very much.

The reasons that the mothers gave for liking or for not liking the 'idea' are shown below. Some mothers gave more than one reason for their answer, some mothers gave no reason.

Reasons for liking the 'idea' Reason	*No. of mothers* *who gave this reason*
(1) the nurse would know more about the mothers particular problems and thus be better able to follow them up	4
(2) it would improve the nurse-patient relationship because mothers would have more confidence in their nurse and find it easier to approach her and ask questions	5
(3) it would reduce the amount of conflicting advice given to the mother	2

Reasons for not liking the 'idea' *(or at least having some reservations)* Reason	*No. of mothers* *who gave this reason*
(1) it might lead to a personality clash between the nurse and her patient	6
(2) if mothers have a choice of nurses then they can go to the one *they* like	3

The Post-change Period

In the post-change period, the mothers who were interviewed were told that the nursing staff on 'their' ward were using a different method of organising their work from other wards in the hospital. They were told that each day a nurse, or group of nurses, was allocated to look after a group of patients. The mothers were all asked if they could identify the nurse, or nurses who had been allocated to look after them on that day (it was possible to verify their responses by checking with the nursing staff).

Twenty-three mothers said that they could identify their 'allocated' nurses and did so. Of these 23, 17 were completely correct. Two mothers had identified one nurse correctly and one nurse incorrectly. In two cases there had in fact been no allocation of staff to patients on that day! In two cases it had been impossible to verify the answers because the mother had been interviewed in the afternoon and the morning staff had all gone off duty.

Seven of the 10 mothers who had not been able to identify their allocated nurse (because they had not known that anyone had been 'allocated' to them) were asked which nurse, or nurses they had seen most often on that day. In four instances the nurses whom the mother had seen most often, had been the ones 'allocated' to look after her. One mother identified one nurse who had been 'allocated' to look after her, and one who had not been. In two instances there had been no allocation of staff on that day!

Did the mothers like the system of patient allocation?

The mothers were all asked if they liked the system of patient allocation. Twenty-six mothers said that they did like it, one mother said that she did not, and six mothers said that they did not think that it mattered very much. The mothers who liked the system of patient allocation were asked to explain why. The reasons the mothers gave, and the number of mothers who gave each reason, are shown below. Some mothers gave more than one reason.

Reasons mothers gave for liking the system of patient allocation	No. of mothers who mentioned each reason
(1) the nurses know about each mothers' problems and follow them up	1
(2) continuity of nursing staff	3
(3) patients and nurses get to know each other better	5
(4) the nurses spend a lot of time with the patients	6
(5) the nurses are easier to approach	3
(6) there is more flexibility in the routine	1

Twenty-two mothers were asked:

"Which nurse would you go to, if you had a problem?"

Of the 22 mothers nine said that they would go to any nurse. Thirteen mothers said that they would go to their allocated nurse (or at least someone whom they had seen a lot of on that day and who they presumed had been allocated to them).

Using the interview data, the mothers were categorised into two groups:

(i) those who liked the system of patient allocation;
(ii) those who either did not like it, or who were ambivalent.

Using the computer, the above groups were cross tabulated with the following sample variables using the Chi-Squared test.

Age; parity; type of delivery; type of room; feeding method; day on which interviewed.

The results suggested that there were no associations significant at the 5% level which linked a liking for the system of patient allocation with any of the above variables tested.

Again, using the computer, the groups of mothers who had liked/not liked/been ambivalent to a system of patient allocation, were cross tabulated with the following groups of mothers (Chi-Squared Test):

(i) Those mothers who had complained of problems/those mothers who had said they had had no problems.
(ii) Those mothers who had felt they were treated as individuals/those mothers who had not felt they were treated as individuals (or had been uncertain).
(iii) Those mothers who had enjoyed their stay in hospital/those mothers who had not enjoyed their stay (or who were uncertain).

The results of the tests showed that there were no associations between these groups which were significant at the 5% level.

Patient allocation and individualised care

Although the association between those mothers who felt they were treated as individuals and those mothers who liked the system of patient allocation was not significant at the 5% level, the majority of mothers who felt that they were treated as individuals also liked the system of patient allocation. However, even had the association been significant at the 5% level, this would not have been surprising since the majority of mothers both felt they were treated as individuals and liked the system of patient allocation and thus no causal relationships could have been suggested. Of more interest and value is the overlap between the reasons that the mothers gave for feeling that they were treated as 'individuals' and the reasons the mothers gave for liking the system of patient allocation.

(f) *The Post-natal Interviews*

Of the mothers who were interviewed in hospital, only 15 in both pre- and post-change periods returned to the post-natal clinic. Some women had wished to visit their own General Practitioner for their post-natal check and some failed to keep their hospital appointment.

The small number who were interviewed at this stage of the research reduces the validity of the comparative analysis. However, in fact there was very little difference in the responses of the two groups of mothers to the questions asked in the interviews. In both the pre- and post-change interviews the consensus of opinion among the mothers was that the care that they had received during the whole of their pregnancy had been very good. The areas mentioned where they would have liked to have seen improvements were:

(i) a reduction in waiting time in the ante-natal clinic;
(ii) more continuity of staff (particularly medical staff) in the ante-natal clinic;
(iii) a reduction in the amount of conflicting advice (in the post-change period one mother said that even seeing two different nurses was one too many!)

In the pre- and post-change periods the majority of mothers felt that enough attention was paid to their emotional needs. Only two mothers, and this was in the post-change period, felt that they could have been given more help when they became upset about a particular problem. The majority of mothers found the nursing staff friendly, approachable and considerate. A number of mothers said that they had not been upset at all. Of interest, however, is the different attitudes that some mothers had to the term 'enough attention'. One mother said that when she was upset she preferred to be alone and was very pleased that both the staff and other patients had left her alone.

The majority of the mothers felt that they were given considerable support from the other patients especially if they were feeling slightly depressed. Women with other children were useful to those mothers who had just had their first child because they could give them some 'tips' about baby care.

There was a lack of agreement about whether the advice that the mothers were given in hospital was useful once the mothers had gone home. In both pre- and post-change periods a few mothers felt that some of the advice that they had been given was useful (for example baby feeding) others felt that once they were at home 'they did their own thing'.

In both pre- and post-change periods, the opinions of the mothers were divided as to whether or not they felt that the time spent in hospital had been useful for establishing a relationship with the baby. A number of mothers, often those with other children, felt that the time spent in hospital had been useful because they could devote all their time to the new baby. However, other mothers felt that this period had not been useful in establishing a relationship with their baby and that when they had gone home they were more able to relax.

(g) *Summary of Results*

The results of the Patient Satisfaction Study suggested that in the areas examined in the pre- and post-change periods:

1. the expectations of all the mothers was generally 'high';
2. those mothers with 'high' expectations found that in general their expectations had been substantiated, while those few mothers who had 'low' expectations found that in general their expectations had been unsubstantiated;
3. the majority of mothers were very satisfied with the care that they had received from the nursing staff during their post-natal stay in hospital.

Thus the results of the study suggested that the system of patient allocation which was introduced into the 'research' ward made little difference to the satisfaction of the mothers with the care that they received in the areas which were examined.

However, there is some evidence that the system of patient allocation which was introduced did make some difference to the mothers perception of the care that they received. In the post-change period there was a significant increase in the number of mothers who said that they had either been looked after by 'just a few nurses' or who said that 'familiar faces kept coming back'. The majority of mothers either liked the system of patient allocation or else did not expressively dislike it. Many of the reasons the mothers gave for liking it, overlapped with the reasons they gave for feeling that they had been treated as 'individuals'.

CHAPTER 7

The Job Satisfaction Study

7.1 Summary of Data Collected

In this part of the study the original intention had been to assess the job satisfaction of the nursing staff working on the 'research' ward and also the nursing staff working on another ward where no change in the organisation of the delivery of care had taken place (the 'control' ward). However, as the study commenced, another ward sister in the hospital expressed a wish to introduce a system of patient allocation into her ward. As it happened this was the ward which had been used to 'pilot' the job satisfaction questionnaire. Since there were few amendments made to the job satisfaction questionnaire which was finally used in the main study, it was decided to use this ward (known as the 'pilot' ward) in the job satisfaction study and so strengthen the research design (see below).

Thus, in the job satisfaction study, job satisfaction was assessed in both the pre- and post-change periods on nursing staff working in the following areas:

(i) the 'research' ward—where the change in the method of organising the delivery of care had taken place and with which the researcher was involved;

(ii) the 'control' ward—where no change in the method of organising the delivery of care had taken place and with which the researcher had no sustained contact;

(iii) the 'pilot' ward—where a change in the method of organising the delivery had taken place but with which the researcher was not involved.

Although the researcher had no official contact with the development of the system of patient allocation on the 'pilot' ward, the communication system among the nursing staff themselves ensured that the two wards developed similar patterns of organisation.

7.2 The Validity of the Design of the Job Satisfaction Study

The main problem in this particular part of the study was to try to separate effects due to the manipulation of the independent variables from those due to being involved in the experiment itself (the Hawthorne effect).

The validity of the research design was reduced by the fact that some of the ward staff, who had their job satisfaction assessed before the change to patient allocation, were different individuals from those who had it assessed after the change. Although the assessment of job satisfaction among the nursing staff on a ward where no change had taken place went some way to improve the strength of the research design, there were many different variables between the two wards which could have affected the reliability of the comparison of job satisfaction for example:

(i) different ward sisters;
(ii) different medical staff;
(iii) different involvement of the researcher.

The inclusion in the study of a ward where a similar change took place but with which the researcher was not involved further strengthened the research design because it made it possible to gain more insight into the effects of the experimental variable and the possible effects of the presence of the researcher. However, it was still not possible to isolate the effects of the experimental variable from the effects of being involved in an experiment. After all, with or without the presence of a researcher on the ward, it is unlikely that the staff would not be aware that their method of organising the delivery of care had been changed, and the results of any analysis must be interpreted in full knowledge of this limitation.

7.3 The Assessment of Job Satisfaction

The job satisfaction of the nursing staff was assessed in both the pre- and post-change periods by using a modified version of a questionnaire originally designed by Mumford (1976) who defined job satisfaction as the fit between what an employee was seeking from work and what he was receiving—in other words the 'fit' between job needs and expectations, and the requirements of the job. Mumford's framework has been used in industrial and commercial organisations for assisting in projects involving job re-design particularly in areas where computer systems were being introduced.

This particular questionnaire was chosen in preference to others because:

(i) it had been designed to be used in areas where a change in the organisation of work had taken place;
(ii) it concentrated on aspects of the job itself and did not include contextual factors such as pay or social facilities;
(iii) it was less structured than many other job satisfaction questionnaires and included some open ended questions.

Mumford's original questionnaire was modified so that it could be used in a nursing context and be completed by all the midwives, nurses and auxiliaries (except sisters) who were working on the chosen maternity wards. Questions referring to computer systems were removed and replaced by questions referring to working with small groups of mothers and babies and planning their care.

The basic structure of the questionnaire was not changed. Job satisfaction was examined along the five variables described by Mumford (1976) and outlined below.

Needs Associated with Personality

1. Knowledge needs
To what extent does the present organisation of work meet the needs of this group of staff for work that fully uses their knowledge and skills. To what extent does it provide them with the opportunity to develop their knowledge and skills more fully.

2. Psychological needs
To what extent does the present organisation of work meet the needs of staff for:

(a) recognition (these are what Herzberg (1966) called 'Motivators');
(b) responsibility;
(c) status;
(d) advancement.

Needs Associated with the Work Role of the Performance of Work Activities

3. Support/Control Needs
To what extent does the work situation provide staff with the kind of support which enables them to carry out their job efficiently.
These support services included:

(a) the provision of necessary information and materials to work at a high level of competence;
(b) supervisory support and the way work is controlled through checks and audits.

4. Task Needs
To what extent does the way in which work is structured and jobs are designed meet staff needs for the following:

(a) the opportunity to use a variety of different skills and different levels of skill;
(b) the opportunity to achieve targets, particularly quality targets, and obtain feedback on how well these targets have been achieved;
(c) autonomy—the opportunity to take decisions, exercise choice, and exert a degree of control over what is done and how it is done.

5. Ethical or Moral Needs

To what extent does management treat employees in the way they think they should be treated. This applies particularly to issues such as communication, consultation and opportunities for participation in decisions which affect employee interest.

Some minor changes were made in the layout and wording of certain questions when it was felt that they were unsuitable or ambiguous in their present form.

Since the purpose of the questionnaire was to obtain information about what the nursing staff thought of various aspects of their job, questions about these various aspects were representative of the five 'needs' described above. Each question contained three main points:

(i) what does the respondent think of the present situation;
(ii) what would the respondent ideally like the situation to be;
(iii) how important is this aspect of the job to him/her.

Also included were general questions about overall job satisfaction, what the respondents liked most about their work and what they liked least.

7.4 The Pilot Study

A small pilot study was carried out using the staff of another ward in the hospital. The aim of the pilot study was to check that the questionnaire could be understood and completed by all grades of staff. Staff were asked to comment on any questions that they found ambiguous or meaningless.

The returned questionnaires suggested that it was a suitable instrument for all grades of staff. Three changes were made in questions wording—a copy of the questionnaire used in the main study can be found in Appendix H.

7.5 The Main Study

(a) *Administration of the Questionnaire*

The revised questionnaires were given to nurses, midwives (excluding the ward sisters) and auxiliaries working on the three wards described above, the 'research' ward the 'control' ward and the 'pilot' ward. The questionnaires were distributed in September/October 1979 and 1980 to all staff who were working on the ward. The researcher approached each staff member individually, the questionnaire was explained and confidentiality was assured. The nursing staff were asked to place the completed questionnaire in a folder which was kept in a locked drawer in the sisters' office. The researcher visited the ward every day and removed any completed questionnaires. Only one member of staff refused to complete the questionnaire. Some questionnaires were not returned because the staff (mainly in training) had either left to work in other hospitals or moved to different areas of the hospital.

In the pre-change period, 22 questionnaires were eventually returned to the researcher; eight in the 'research' ward, seven from the 'pilot' ward and seven from the 'control' ward. In the post-change period 32 questionnaires were returned; 13 from the 'research' ward, 12 from the 'pilot' ward and seven from the 'control' ward. A total of 54 questionnaires was obtained. Details of the various grades of nursing staff who completed the questionnaires are shown in Table 15.

TABLE 15

Grades and Numbers of Nursing Staff who Completed the Job Satisfaction Questionnaires on each Ward in the Pre- and Post-Change Periods

'Pilot Ward'	Pre	Post
Nursing Auxiliary	2	1
Nursery Nurse	2	1
Staff Midwife	—	2
Enrolled Nurse	—	—
Pupil Midwife	2	2
Student Midwife	1	1
Total	7	7

'Control Ward'	Pre	Post
Nursing Auxiliary	2	3
Nursery Nurse	1	1
Staff Midwife	1	2
Enrolled Nurse	1	1
Pupil Midwife	1	3
Student Midwife	1	2
Total	7	12

'Research Ward'	Pre	Post
Nursing Auxiliary	3	2
Nursery Nurse	1	1
Staff Midwife	1	2
Enrolled Nurse	—	—
Pupil Midwife	1	5
Student Midwife	2	3
Total	8	13

(b) *Analysis of Data*

The main purpose of the questionnaire was to acquire a data base from which job satisfaction in the pre- and post-change periods could be assessed and any differences explored further. However, the use of different types of questions in the questionnaire, (ordinal, nominal and open-ended) made it impractical to obtain a single individual score of job satisfaction. Thus, the responses to the questionnaires were analysed in two ways:

(i) by using a factor analysis technique on the questions which had an ordinal scale;

(ii) by considering responses to the other questions separately.

(c) *The Factor Analysis*

In this study factor analysis was used to simplify the data and explore any inter-relationships between the various questions. All pre- and post-change questionnaires were used in the factor analysis (N = 54). A question referring to overall job satisfaction (Q21) was excluded from the factor analysis but was used for the purpose of comparison between the various wards.

(i) *The results of the factor analysis*

The factor analysis gave five distinct factors where a meaningful pattern of 'significant' factor loadings emerged. Five factors explained 53·5% of the variance. In this study because of the comparatively small sample size (N = 54) factor loadings above ± 0.40 were considered to be significant. The questions which had significant factor loadings on each of the five factors were grouped together and a label was applied to each factor. This label attempted to explain the nature of the question groups falling into each factor. Questions 15A, 15B and 16 did not have a significant factor loading (that is greater than ± 0.40) on any of the five factors and, therefore, were not included in any of the factor explanations. The questions which constituted each factor are shown in Table 16 together with the significant factor loading. A brief explanation of each factor and the label applied to each are discussed below:

Factor 1
This factor contained all the responses to questions relating to knowledge and psychological needs:

The Intrinsic Satisfaction Factor

Factor 2
This factor contained mainly the questions relating to the system of patient allocation:

The Patient Allocation Factor

TABLE 16
Questions (and Factor Loadings) Constituting Each Factor

FACTOR 1		FACTOR 2		FACTOR 3	
Questions	Loading	Questions	Loading	Questions	Loading
1C	(0·56)	9A	−(0·41)	12A	(0·78)
2A	(0·73)	19A	(0·55)	12B	(0·77)
2C	(0·69)	19B	−(0·44)	13A	(0·85)
3A	(0·73)	20A	(0·90)	13B	(0·88)
3C	(0·54)	20B	−(0·82)	18A	(0·55)
4A	(0·68)	20C	(0·80)	—	—
4B	(0·59)	—	—	—	—
5A	(0·52)	—	—	—	—
5B	(0·70)	—	—	—	—
6A	−(0·59)	—	—	—	—
7	−(0·56)	—	—	—	—
11C	(0·60)	—	—	—	—

FACTOR 4		FACTOR 5	
Questions	Loading	Questions	Loading
8	−(0·60)	1A	(0·75)
9A	−(0·57)	5A	−(0·65)
9B	(0·54)	11A	−(0·56)
10B	(0·57)	14	−(0·56)
17A	−(0·66)	—	—
17B	(0·40)	—	—
18B	(0·67)	—	—

Factor 3
This factor contained mainly questions relating to job interdependence:

The Interdependence Factor

Factor 4
This factor contained mainly the questions about job autonomy and amount of supervision:

The Autonomy Factor

Factor 5
This factor was less clear cut than the others but seemed mainly to involve questions relating to the amount of influence the nurse had in her job:

The Influence Factor

Although the five factors isolated did not correspond with the five contractual areas outlined by Mumford (1976) (perhaps because some questions could have been attributed to more than one category) there is a clear distinction between psychological/knowledge needs and support control and task needs. All the knowledge and psychological need questions were in Factor 1.

(ii) *The relationship of the factors to overall job satisfaction*
The assessment of the overall job satisfaction of the individual respondent was obtained from the results of the question:

"Taking your job as a whole, how much job satisfaction does it provide you with . . .?" (Question 21).

The distribution of responses is shown in Table 17.

TABLE 17
Assessment of Overall Job Satisfaction

	Number of responses (Total Sample)
'a great deal	14
'quite a lot'	19
'a moderate amount'	16
'very little'	2
'hardly any at all'	2
Total	53

(1 missing value)

Factor scores for each of five factors described above were obtained for each individual respondent. The Kruskal-Wallis one way analysis of variance was used to test for any significant differences between respondents factor score on each of the five factors, and their assessment of overall job satisfaction.

The results of the test indicated that only the scores on Factor 1 were significantly associated with assessment of overall job satisfaction ($p = 0.0003$).

Thus the study does not support Mumford's theory that task needs and support/control needs are important for job satisfaction. However, it does lend support to other studies of job satisfaction among nursing staff which have suggested that the 'intrinsic' aspects of the job play an important part in the job satisfaction of nurses (Redfern, 1979; Austin, 1978; Everly and Falcioni, 1976; Hockey, 1976).

(d) *Differences in Job Satisfaction Between the Wards in the Pre- and Post-Change Periods*

This was assessed in two ways:

(i) by using the overall job satisfaction scores;
(ii) by using the individual factor scores of Factor 1.

The overall job satisfaction scores by ward and period of change are shown in Table 18. Each response category was given a numerical value 'a great deal' = 5, to 'hardly any at all = 1. The Kruskal-Wallis two way analysis of variance was used to test for any significant differences in the results between the wards in the pre- and post-change periods. The results suggested that there were *no* significant differences either between the wards or between the pre- and post-change periods.

TABLE 18

The Overall Job Satisfaction Scores by Ward and Period of Change

Assessment of overall job satisfaction Pre-change	Pilot Ward	Control Ward	Research Ward
'a great deal	1	3	2
'quite a lot'	2	3	3
'a moderate amount'	3	1	3
'very little'	—	—	—
'hardly any at all'	1	—	—

Assessment of overall job satisfaction Post-change	Pilot Ward	Control Ward	Research Ward
'a great deal'	4	2	2
'quite a lot'	3	3	5
'a moderate amount'	—	3	6
'very little'	—	2	—
'hardly any at all'	—	1	—

(1 missing value)

When the distribution of the scores shown in Table 18 was examined more closely it appeared that the greatest changes had occurred on the 'control' ward and the 'pilot' ward. On the 'pilot' ward high satisfaction appeared to have increased in the post-change period and low satisfaction had decreased. On the 'control' ward low satisfaction had increased in the post-change period. On the 'research' ward there was little difference. It is important to remember that *no* change in work organisation had taken place on the 'control' ward.

(ii) The individual factor scores for Factor 1 were grouped into the same categories as shown in Table 18. The Kruskal-Wallis two way analysis of variance was used to test for significant differences. The results suggested that there were no significant differences at the 5% level between the wards or between the pre- and post-change periods.

(e) *Other Differences Between the Wards in the Pre- and Post-change Periods*

In a similar manner to that described above for Factor 1, analysis of the variance of the individual factor scores of factors 2, 3, 4 and 5 was carried out between the wards in the pre- and post-change period using the Kruskal-Wallis two way test. The results suggested that:

(i) There was a significant difference in Factor 2 (the patient allocation factor) between the wards at the 5% level ($0.05 > p > 0.02$) and between the pre- and post-change periods at the 1% level ($0.01 > p > 0.0001$).

(ii) There was a significant difference at the 5% level in Factor 3 (the interdependence factor) between the wards ($0.05 > p > 0.02$) but no difference between the pre- and post-change periods.

(iii) There were no significant differences in Factor 4 (the autonomy factor) or Factor 5 (the influence factor) either between the wards or between the pre- and post-change periods.

The significant differences in Factor 2 are not surprising since the research study was set up to effect such a change but it lends a little credibility to the usefulness of the factor analysis technique. In Factor 3 the same differences between the wards in the pre-change period were also present in the post-change period.

(f) *The Nursing Staff's Opinion of the System of Patient Allocation*

In the questionnaire the nursing staff were asked:

"Do you ever get the chance to look after or help a small group of mothers and babies rather than all the mothers of all the babies?"

If they replied 'Yes' they were asked if they liked it. If they replied 'No' they were asked if they would like to work like that.

In the pre-change period the majority of nursing staff said they did not work in that way but would like to try it. In the post-change period, on the 'research' ward and 'pilot' ward most of the nurses said they worked in this way and nearly all claimed to like it. On the 'control' ward most of the nurses said they never worked in this way, but all but one said they would like the opportunity to do so.

In the questionnaire, respondents were not asked *why* they liked the new system of patient allocation, however, this had already been discussed in the staff interviews. During these interviews most nurses and midwives claimed to like the system of Patient Allocation, although there were exceptions. Among the reasons for liking it were:

(i) the staff felt they knew more about the mothers and they felt that teamwork between the nurses working together was good;
(ii) they could envisage their work-load better and could plan their work accordingly.

(g) *The Analysis of the Open-ended Questions*

For the purpose of comparing differences in the job satisfaction of the nursing staff the 'open-ended' questions did not prove to be a useful measure of the differences in job satisfaction between the wards and in the pre- and post-change periods. Because the number of respondents in each ward was small and because there was considerable variation in the responses to the 'open-ended' questions it was not possible to establish any meaningful differences in the pattern of responses between the different grades of staff in the pre- and post-change periods. However, the responses to some of the questions are interesting in that they highlight some of the areas of work which are important to the various members of staff regardless of the methods used to organise the delivery of care on the respective wards.

In this respect, of particular interest were the responses to questions:

Q24—"what do you like most about your work?"
Q23—"what do you like least about your work?"
Q3(b)—"what gives you most sense of achievement?"

Q24—"what do you like most about your work?"
In both the pre- and post-change periods the responses to these questions fall into three categories:

Category 1—Aspects relating to the nurse, for example feelings of personal well being (that is feeling worthwhile/useful).
Opportunities for personal development (for example education responsibility).
Opportunities to use skills.

Category 2—Aspects relating to patients, for example giving care to mothers and babies.
Establishing relationships with the patients.
Teaching the mothers.
Seeing the mothers recover and go home.
Being able to spend more time with the patients.

Category 3—Contextual aspects, for example good staff relationships.
Organisation or work.

Multi-disciplinary approach.
Variety of work.
The amount of autonomy in the work (that is not too much close supervision).

The number of responses which fall into the three categories on each ward in the pre- and post-change periods are shown below in Table 19. Some respondents gave more than one reason, some respondents did not answer the question.

TABLE 19
Responses to the Question "What Do You Like Most About Your Work?"

	'Control' Ward		'Pilot' Ward		'Research' Ward	
	Pre	Post	Pre	Post	Pre	Post
Category 1	1	6	1	8	2	9
Category 2	10	13	7	3	8	9
Category 3	3	2	2	6	5	6

In the 'control' ward the responses falling into Category 2 (aspects relating to the patient) remained high in both pre- and post-change periods. On the 'pilot' ward and the 'research' ward although responses falling into category 2 were high in the pre-change period, in the post-change period the number of responses falling into this category had dropped comparatively (and numerically on the 'pilot' ward). Responses falling into Category 1 (aspects relating to the nurse) had risen on all the wards in the post-change period but responses falling into Category 3 had risen only in the 'pilot' ward and the 'research' ward in the post-change period. Responses relating to the liking for the method of organising the ward was only mentioned once in the pre-change period—by a staff nurse working on the 'control' ward. Whereas in the post-change period it was mentioned five times by respondents, mainly pupil midwives working on the 'research' ward and the 'pilot' ward.

Q23—"What do you like least about your work?"
In both the pre- and post-change periods responses to this question fell mainly into Category 3 (contextual aspects) which was described above. However, this Category was expanded to include items such as:

Pay; Hours of work; Amount of paperwork; Shortage of staff; Lack of communication.

A few responses fell into Category 1 (aspects relating to the nurse) but only one fell into Category 2 (aspects relating to the patient).

The number of responses which fell into each category on each ward in the pre- and post-change period are shown below in Table 20. Some respondents gave more than one answer to the question, some respondents gave no answer.

TABLE 20
Responses to the Question "What Do You Like Least About Your Work?"

	'Control' Ward		'Pilot' Ward		'Research' Ward	
	Pre	Post	Pre	Post	Pre	Post
Category 1	1	5	3	1	1	4
Category 2	—	—	—	—	1	—
Category 3	5	8	7	7	11	9

Within Category 3 aspects relating to the organisation of work (for example, work routines, traditional methods, task/patient allocation) were mentioned as aspects which nurses liked *least* about their work, only on the 'pilot' ward and the 'research' ward in the pre-change period. In the post-change period these same aspects were mentioned on all three wards.

Within Category 2, aspects relating to the lack of opportunity for personal development were mentioned in the post-change period, mainly on the 'control' ward and on the 'research' ward, and mainly by nurses in training grades, for example, pupil midwives/student nurses.

Q3b—"What gives you most sense of achievement at work?"
In many respects the responses to this question were similar to responses to Q24 (What do you like *most* about your work?). The responses to Q3(b) fell into two distinct categories; those relating to the personal development of the nurse (Category 1) and those relating to patient care (Category 2). Among the items mentioned which

TABLE 21
Responses to the Question "What Gives you Most Sense of Achievement at Work?"

	'Control' Ward		'Pilot' Ward		'Research' Ward	
	Pre	Post	Pre	Post	Pre	Post
Category 1	3	6	—	3	2	4
Category 2	8	7	5	6	6	14

related to the personal development of the nurse were aspects relating to:

'getting all the work done'
being able to complete a 'task' by oneself
'coping' with a difficult situation
feeling a valued and useful member of a team
application of, or acquisition of knowledge.

Among the items relating to patient care were aspects relating to:

good patient outcomes (that is seeing the mother recover and go home).

developing a relationship with a mother
teaching the mothers how to care for their babies
the actual giving of care and solving problems.

The number of responses which fell into each category on each ward in the pre- and post-change periods are shown opposite in Table 21.

It appears that in both pre- and post-change periods the majority of respondents gained most of their sense of achievement from their contact with the patients.

(h) *Summary of Results*

The results of the questionnaire suggested that although the nursing staff who were using the system of patient allocation liked it, there was little evidence to suggest that the change to patient allocation had much effect upon the overall measurement of job satisfaction, or upon the various factors related to the job satisfaction of the nursing staff.

CHAPTER 8

Discussion, Explanations and Implications of the Results

8.1 Summary of the Results

The results of the observation study suggested that there were very few differences in the observed behaviour and activities of the nursing staff. Those changes of any significance which were observed occurred mainly on shift 1.

Although the majority of patients said that they liked the system of patient allocation which was introduced, there did not appear to be any noticeable increase in the overall satisfaction of the patients with their care. However, both before and after the change the majority of patients were very satisfied with the care that they had received.

Although the majority of nurses and midwives said that they liked the system of patient allocation which was introduced, there did not appear to be any increase in the pre- and post-change measurements of job satisfaction. Job satisfaction among the nursing staff was high, both before and after the change.

The majority of the nurses and midwives said that their relationship with the mothers had improved and certainly there were some changes in the initiating factors of nurse patient interaction which may have indicated a change in the nurse patient relationship. There was, however, little difference in the total amount of time that the nursing staff spent interacting with the mothers.

Although the majority of the nursing staff said that they liked the system of patient allocation which was introduced, not all did so. One member of staff, the nursery nurse, felt that it diminished her work role.

The results of the study suggested very strongly that although the nursing staff seemed to like the system of patient allocation which was introduced, it made little difference to patient satisfaction. The results obtained in this study are similar to those obtained by Auld (1968), Chavasse (1978) and Boekholdt and Kanters (1978).

8.2 Explanations and Conjectures

Were the nursing staff actually using the system of patient allocation when the post-change data were collected?

The possibility was considered that the reason there were so few significant differences between the pre- and post-change periods was because the nursing staff were not really using a system of patient allocation at all. The data, particularly that of the observation study, were re-examined to explore this possibility.

As described in Chapter 6, the system of patient allocation which was introduced consisted of three parts:

(i) the planning and recording system;
(ii) associated practices;
(iii) the allocation itself.

The extent to which the nursing staff were using each part of the new system when the post-change observations were being undertaken is described below.

(i) *The planning and recording system*

All the planning and recording instruments used previously were discontinued. Thus there was no alternative but to use the new ones. The tendency to have a task list (hidden in a drawer) was curtailed by the nursing officer in charge of the ward.

(ii) *The associated practices*

Whenever possible the nurses and midwives would look after a group of patients for consecutive periods of duty. However, the shift system coupled with unexpected sickness absence, meant that it was not always possible for a nurse to be with the same group of patients for a long period. In addition, after a few shifts of caring for one group the nursing staff often became anxious about "not knowing the other patients". On most occasions, the morning staff all attended the lunchtime report and each team leader gave the report on her own patients. Sometimes the sister or nurse in charge gave a report to the evening staff at 4.00 pm before she went off duty. Generally at least one team member went with the medical staff when they did a 'business round' of her patients.

A practice which was invariably carried out was the 'nursing round' of the patients by each team (or at least some members of it) each morning after report. Other practices, however, were still frequently carried out on a whole ward basis, for example giving medications and stocking up patients' lockers. Bedmaking and observations were usually carried out on a team basis.

(iii) *The allocation itself*

In the nursing staff observation study, eight early shifts were observed in the post-change period. In seven cases the nurses were allocated to one of the two groups of patients. The exception was one sister (sister

91

A) who remained in overall charge of the ward during her span of duty. Eight afternoon shifts were observed but in only three instances was any attempt made to allocate the staff coming on duty at 1.00 pm. These three instances involved a sister, a junior pupil midwife and a student nurse.

The data were examined to assess the number of interactions the individual observed nurses had with each patient. In the post-change period the number of interactions each had with both their allocated group of patients and their non-allocated group were expressed as percentages of their total number of interactions. Table 22 shows the percentages and numbers of interactions in shift 1 post-change, that each nurse had with both allocated and non-allocated patients. When there was no allocation of staff, patients were grouped according to the divisions usually used for allocation and the numbers and percentages of interaction calculated for each group (for example for sister A).

TABLE 22

Interactions with Allocated and Non-allocated Patients in Shift 1 Post-change

	Allocated Group		Non-Allocated Group	
	%	N	%	N
Sister B	75%	63	25%	21
Staff Midwife	78%	38	22%	11
Pupil Midwife (A)	85%	47	15%	8
Pupil Midwife (B)	86%	59	14%	10
Student Nurse	84%	61	16%	12
Nursery Nurse	70%	23	30%	10
Nursing Auxiliary	90%	46	10%	5
	Bed 1–7		Bed 8–13	
Sister A	54%	(29)	46%	(25)

When the nurses were allocated to a group of patients on shift one, they spent an average of 81% of their interactions with these patients. Table 23 shows the percentages and numbers of interactions spent in shift two by each nurse, with patients grouped according to the divisions usually used for allocation. In shift two, when there was no allocation of staff, the ratio of interaction between the two patient groups was 58% : 42%. When there was an attempt at allocation the ratio was 52% : 48%.

Thus in shift two, the attempts at allocation had little effect upon the distribution of nurse patient interaction.

TABLE 23
Interactions with Allocated and Non-allocated Patients in Shift 2 Post-change

	Beds 1–7		Beds 8–13	
	%	(N)	%	(N)
Sister A	51%	38	49%*	37
Sister B	61%	50	39%	32
Staff Midwife	52%	45	48%	42
Pupil Midwife A	46%	31	54%	37
Pupil Midwife B	56%*	50	44%	39
Student Nurse	50%	23	50%*	23
Nursery Nurse	63%	36	37%	21
Nursing Auxiliary	67%	27	33%	13

* Nurse Allocated to this Group

For comparison, the mothers with whom the nurses interacted in the pre-change period were grouped into the divisions usually used for allocation in the post-change period. Table 24 shows the percentages and numbers of interactions falling into each group.

The data displayed in Tables 22, 23 and 24 suggest that when there was no allocation of staff to patients, the nurses tended to divide their time equally among all the patients. When there was allocation, the nurses tended (but only on shift 1) to spend most of their time with the group to whom they had been allocated.

The nursing staff observation study suggested that when nurses and midwives were allocated to a group of patients, they had approximately 80% of their interactions with that group. The results

TABLE 24
Interaction with Patients in Shifts 1 and 2 Pre-change

	Shift 1				Shift 2			
	1–7		8–13		1–7		8–13	
	%	(N)	%	(N)	%	(N)	%	(N)
Sister	64%	49	51%	27	51%	26	49%	25
Staff Midwife	36%	24	64%	42	65%	52	35%	28
Pupil Midwife A	52%	44	48%	40	51%	42	49%	41
Pupil Midwife B	45%	37	55%	45	33%	32	67%	64
Student Nurse	49%	32	51%	33	67%	36	33%	18
Nursery Nurse	79%	38	21%	10	39%	35	61%	54
Nursing Auxiliary	88%	43	12%	6	67%	27	33%	13

also suggested that there was no difference in the percentage of observed time spent with the patients in the pre- and post-change period (approximately 30% of observed time in both cases). Thus one would expect that when staff were allocated to a group of patients, the 30% of observed time would now be being spent primarily with, for example, 12 patients instead of 24 and that in the patient observation study this would be reflected in the interactions between nursing staff and patients. One would expect that when staff were allocated to patients, the percentage of interactions from one or two nurses would be high, with perhaps a small percentage of interactions from other staff members. When there was no allocation of staff one would expect each patient to receive a more equal division of the percentage of interaction from each of the staff members on duty.

Table 25 shows the percentage of total nurse patient interaction time for each observed mother, which was given by the allocated nurses on shift 1 of the post-change period.

However, Table 26 shows the percentage of total nurse patient interaction time given in shift one of the pre-change period (when there was no allocation of staff to patients) by the 2, and then the 3, most frequently interacting nurses.

The data displayed in Tables 25 and 26 suggest that in this study, from the mothers' perspective the allocation of specific nurses to care for them did not mean that on any one day the mothers had a greater percentage of their care given by a particular nurse or group of nurses, than when there had been no such allocation. Neither did it seem to decrease the number of nurses interacting with each mother. On only two occasions in shift 1 post-change did the mother not interact with all the nursing staff on duty on that shift, compared to one occasion in the pre-change period.

Thus the answer to the question 'were the nursing staff really using the system of patient allocation?' would appear to be that they were—

TABLE 25

Percentage of Nurse-Patient Interaction Time Given by Nursing Staff Allocated to Each Individual Mother in Shift 1 of the Post-change Period

(Patients identified by code number)

Patient	% Care given by allocated nurses	Number of nurses allocated
203	68%	3
204	93%	3
206	96%	4
209	80%	2
212	69%	2

TABLE 26

Percentage of Nurse-Patient Interaction Time Given by the (2) and the (3) Members of the Nursing Staff who Interacted Most Frequently with the Observed Mothers

(Patients identified by code number)

Patient	% Care given by 2 nurses	% Care given by 3 nurses
108	59%	76%
110	91%	94%
111	87%	99%
101	87%	93%
103	74%	79%
106	46%	66%

but mainly on shift 1. Furthermore, while the change seemed to affect the experience of the nursing staff in that they spent 80% of their time with their allocated patients it did not appear to have so much effect upon the experience of the mothers. In the post-change period the mothers still had the same pattern of contact with the nursing staff as they had had in the pre-change period. These findings go a long way to explain why the nursing staff appeared to like the system of patient allocation but that the mothers did not seem to notice much difference. In retrospect it would have been useful to have obtained some measure of the continuity of the system of patient allocation by, for example, recording the number of consecutive shifts that a particular nurse or midwife cared for the same group of mothers. It is possible that in the pre-change period, although on any one day a particular mother received most of her care from one or two particular staff members, for the remainder of her stay she may have had little contact with them. In the post-change period, however, she may have received most of her care from the same members of the nursing staff for a number of days.

Were the changes which did occur a result of the introduction of the system of patient allocation?

The limitations of each area of data collection have been explained at various points in this volume. However, the number of different methods used, and the extent to which the finding of each are consistent with the findings of the others, can be used to support or reject various explanations. This technique was described by Denzin (1970) as 'data triangulation'.

In the observation study most of the significant differences in the observed parameters of the pre- and post-change periods occurred in

95

shift 1 and it was established that the nursing staff were allocated to patients mainly on shift one. However, there were a few significant differences which occurred in shift 2 but only on two occasions were members of the nursing staff allocated to the patients on shift 2 of the post-change period. One explanation for the existence of significant differences when there was no allocation of staff may lie in the fact that the system of patient allocation which was introduced consisted of three parts:

the allocation of nursing staff to patients
associated practices
the new planning and recording system.

Some of the observed significant differences which occurred on shift two, may have been due to effects of the planning recording system and the associated practices which were introduced. For example, some of the changes in the initiating factor categories of the nurse patient interaction may have resulted from the nursing staff spending a greater percentage of their time in ward report or on medical ward rounds.

In Chapter 4 it was mentioned that when using the new system of patient allocation, many of the nurses and midwives interviewed said that they seemed to know more about the patients. This is not surprising since it appears that they were likely to have been receiving more information. This increased knowledge would not disappear at the end of each shift.

Another example of the side effects of the system of patient allocation causing significant difference in shift 2 may have been the increase in the post-change period of interactions initiated by the category 'clinical'. This could be indicating that the tradition of "getting everything done by lunch time" was being broken down by a generally more flexible approach to organising the work of the ward.

In shift 1 post-change, there was a significant increase in the percentage of time that the nursing staff spent in the category 'communication', which was caused primarily by an increased percentage of time spent in ward report and an increased percentage of time spent 'attending medical ward rounds'. Changes in these practices had been deliberately introduced by the system of patient allocation.

One initiating factor category which figured prominently in the significant changes was 'category D', which entailed activities involving:

nurse asking mother for information
nurse giving mother information
mother asking nurse for information.

In shift 1 in the nursing staff observation study, the nurse initiated interactions initiated by this factor tended to be lower in the post-change period. Either the nursing staff were initiating their interactions by asking the patients for information less frequently, or else they were initiating fewer interactions with the specific intent of giving the patient certain pieces of information. In shift 2 of the patient observation study, in the post-change period significantly less interactions appeared to have been initiated by the initiating factor category D. Possible explanations for these changes can be found in the 'associated practices' which were introduced as part of the system of patient allocation.

In Chapter 3 it was described how, after the early morning report, the nursing staff visited each of their respective allocated patients. This activity was categorised as surveillance (category C) because the nurses and midwives were 'checking' each patient. However, during this interaction the nursing staff discussed with each individual mother her and her baby's care for that day. For example, they would ascertain the best time to bath the baby, which would fit in with that particular baby's feeding pattern and yet not result in congestion in the nursery bath area. In addition, they enquired generally about the health and progress of all the mothers and babies in their care. During this time they gave the mothers and received from them, a considerable amount of information. This could have meant that during the remainder of the shift, either requests for this information or specific intentions to give this information would not be used to initiate subsequent interaction.

Reductions in initiating factor category D in the nurse initiated interactions could have been caused by the nursing staff initiating less interactions by:

(a) giving the patient information
(b) asking the patients for information.

In this study no attempt had been made to differentiate between these two types of interaction and in retrospect it would have been useful to have collected more data on the pattern of information giving and receiving between the nursing staff and the patients. However, during the course of the observation studies, in particular the patient observation study, it had appeared to the researcher that members of the nursing staff tended to ask the mother for information *less often* and this affected categorisation of the initiating factor of some interactions. For example, in the pre-change period, towards the end of the morning, a member of the nursing staff carrying the daily work book, would enter the four bed bay in which the researcher was observing. She would ask all the patients in turn if they had had a bath/shower and tick the appropriate column in the book. In the post-change period this did not happen—partly because there was no longer a work book, but partly because the nurse or midwife allocated to the patient was more likely to say to her "have you had your bath yet?" It was obvious to the researcher that the nurse or midwife knew what particular form of ablution the particular mother had been going to have and thus she was 'checking' to see if she had had it. Interactions initiated in such a manner were coded as 'C' (surveillance). The fact that the nursing staff claimed to know more about the patients, the fact that more time was spent in ward reports and the fact that the nursing staff gave the patients a considerable amount of information when they visited them after the 7.45 am ward report would tend to support the observation that interactions initiated by category D were significantly reduced in the post-change period and that this reduction was likely to have been caused by the nursing staff *asking* the patient for information less frequently.

The increase in the number and percentage of nurse initiated interactions in shift 1 of the post-change period in the patient observation study may be seen as a reflection of claims made by the nursing staff in the interview and discussed in Chapter 4. Some of the nurses and midwives interviewed said that they felt more responsible for their patients when they were specifically allocated to a group of them and that they found it easier to envisage their workload, with the result that they could plan their work better and did not feel quite so harassed as they had previously. Taken together, these comments by the staff members may help to explain the increased number of interactions initiated by factors categorised as 'surveillance' which occurred in shift 1 of the post-change period. The patients who were allocated to a specific group of nurses and midwives were the responsibility of those nurses and midwives; if *they* did not 'check' on them no one else would. Moreover, having a smaller number of patients to care for would make it easier for the nurses and midwives to remember which patients they needed to 'check' on and for what reason, and make it less likely that they would be side-tracked by some other activity.

These findings of the observation study examined in the context of other data suggest that there were some differences between the pre- and post-change periods which were likely to have been caused by the change to the system of patient allocation. The question which must now be asked is: "Why did these changes have so little effect upon patient satisfaction and staff job satisfaction?"

Patient Satisfaction

Two possible explanations can be put forward to explain why the system of patient allocation which was introduced had so little effect upon patient satisfaction. The first is a methodological limitation, and the second is the possibility that the methods the nursing staff use to deliver care are not important determinants of patient satisfaction.

Methodological limitations

When the methodological limitations of the study are considered two factors must be discussed:

(i) were the research instruments suitable for the purpose for which they were intended (that is did they collect relevant data);
(ii) were the areas examined the 'correct ones'.

(i) In the patient satisfaction study, both interviews and questionnaires were used, and both methods have disadvantages and advantages. The results of the 'expectation' questionnaire suggested that the majority of mothers had high expectations of care. This does not support suggestions from other researchers (Perkins, 1978; Cartwright, 1964) that one of the reasons for high levels of patient satisfaction with care that professionals often consider inadequate is the fact that patients have 'low' expectations. However, it is consistent with the evidence presented by Kitzinger (1979) that the particular hospital where the research was undertaken was considered to be a 'good' one. The mothers who were most likely to expect to enjoy their stay in hospital were those who had had a previous confinement at the hospital and presumably their expectations were based on previous experience. It is also possible that many of the respondents, especially those who were expecting their first child, did not state what they had 'expected' but what they had 'hoped for'. This possibility had been anticipated and had been discussed with the respondents when the questionnaires were distributed. Unfortunately, this does not mean that the instructions were adhered to.

The results of the expectation survey suggested that a number of mothers were 'inconsistent' about their expectations. While this inconsistency may have been due to poor questionnaire design, it is also possible that since 'expectations' are often nebulous and difficult to define, this may have been reflected in the questionnaire responses.

In the interviews, the mothers spoke freely about their experiences. The fact that the researcher had met them all before in the ante-natal clinic reduced the difficulties of establishing a good rapport during the interviews.

(ii) The research instruments were used to collect data in specific areas of care. The results of the study suggested that there were no, or at best very little, differences in patient satisfaction with care in those areas, in the pre- and post-change periods. This does not mean that the system of patient allocation which was introduced made no difference to the mothers satisfaction with *all* care. It merely means that in the *areas examined* there was no difference. It is possible that if different areas were examined differences would be manifested. However, this study was designed to examine the areas of care which were reputed to be improved by a system of patient allocation. These areas of care centred mainly around the psycho-social aspects of care and it was these areas that the research instruments were designed to examine. If these are not the areas of care which are affected by the introduction of a system of patient allocation, that is not a fault of the research instruments.

The possibility that the methods the nursing staff use to deliver care is not an important determinant of patient satisfaction

The results of the observation study suggested that the amount of contact that the individual mothers had with the nursing staff during the hours of 7.45 am–9.30 pm is comparatively short (Table 7). Patient satisfaction on the other hand is likely to be based on the whole period of the hospital stay. It is possible that the method the nursing staff use to deliver care is only one factor among many which can influence patient satisfaction and for many people it may be comparatively unimportant. Of more importance in maternity wards may be such factors as rooming-in, demand feeding, good food, clean toilets, flexible visiting hours and pleasant nursing staff (who remember the mothers' names) and the attitude and behaviour of the medical staff. These factors are not dependent upon the existence of a system of patient allocation.

Job Satisfaction

Any meaningful explanations of the results of the job satisfaction study ultimately depend on whether the questionnaire was an adequate discriminatory instrument. When the questionnaire was administered it was pointed out to the nursing staff that it only referred to the particular ward that they were working on at that time. While it would be comparatively easy for the more permanent members of the nursing staff to follow this instruction, the junior staff who tended to rotate onto other wards in the hospital may have found it more difficult to separate their experience of one ward with their experience of the hospital in general. This of course would reduce the validity of the questionnaire as a discriminatory instrument. The possible explanations for the results which are discussed below, depend on the assumption that the questionnaire was an adequate discriminatory instrument and that the nurses and midwives who completed it did so honestly and followed the instructions they were given.

In this study job satisfaction was measured in two ways:

(i) by self-reported overall job satisfaction
(ii) by individual factor scores of Factor 1.

The results of the pre- and post-change inter-ward comparisons for each measure were slightly different. One explanation for this could be that they were measuring different things. In the literature on the measurement of job satisfaction, it has been suggested by Cameron (1973) that both overall satisfaction scores and facet satisfaction scores should be used because when there is a discrepancy between the two sets of scores some of it is due to facets not included in the questionnaire and there is some variance, other than error variance, in overall satisfaction that cannot be predicted from facet satisfaction.

In this study, the aspects of the system of patient allocation that the nurses claimed to like, could have been included in their overall assessment of job satisfaction and it is possible that this may account for the differences in the results.

The results of the two measures of job satisfaction are discussed separately.

The Overall Satisfaction Scores

The results suggested that in the post-change period high job satisfaction increased as one of the wards which changed to patient allocation—the 'pilot' ward. Low job satisfaction increased on the 'control' ward in the post-change period and in the 'research' ward everything remained much the same.

It it was the change to patient allocation which caused the rise in job satisfaction on the 'pilot' ward, why did a similar rise not occur on the 'research' ward? And why did *low* job satisfaction increase on the 'control' ward when there had been *no* change in the post-change period?

It is possible that the change in job satisfaction on the 'pilot' ward is no more than a 'Hawthorne effect' generated by the excitement of being involved in a pioneering new venture.

Is it also possible that the increase in *low* job satisfaction on the 'control' ward is a kind of *reverse* 'Hawthorne effect' generated by *not* being involved in a pioneering new venture? (There were five maternity wards in the hospital. By the time the post-change questionnaire was administered, two wards had changed to patient allocation reasonably successfully, two wards were 'tinkering' and the only ward which had not experimented with the new system was the 'control' ward where the ward sister was particularly hostile to the idea of patient allocation. Junior staff rotated round the hospital wards as part of their training and would have experienced the new system on other wards.)

However, this does not explain why job satisfaction did not rise in the 'research' ward. A possible explanation could be that at the time the post-change questionnaire was administered there was a certain amount of unrest on the ward caused by changes in the senior ward staff. On the other wards the sisters and some senior part-time staff midwives had been in post for some years. But, if this is an acceptable explanation it only serves to reduce the evidence that a change in the organisation of work is an important enough event to overcome other factors which influence job satisfaction.

The Factor Scores

The aspects of the nurse's job measured by the factor scores of Factors 1, 3, 4 and 5 (responsibility, achievement, challenge, level of decision making, amount of supervision) were unchanged between wards and in the pre- and post-change periods. These results suggest that these facets of the job are unrelated to the system of patient allocation. Among the reputed advantages of a system of patient allocation are claims that it would result in the nursing staff having increased responsibility, decision making, variety and use of skills and knowledge. In this study it did not appear to. However, both *before* and *after* the change, the majority of the nursing staff reported high satisfaction with most job facets.

It is possible that there was little difference in the job satisfaction of the nursing staff because the changes to a system of patient allocation made little difference to the work of the nursing staff. However, the results obtained in the observation study and the patient satisfaction study suggest that there were some differences, albeit small. Furthermore, when asked both in the questionnaire and in the interviews the majority of the nursing staff said that they did like the system of patient allocation. In the interviews the nursing staff said that they liked it because:

(i) The staff felt that they knew more about the mothers.
(ii) They felt that teamwork between the nurses and midwives working together had improved.
(iii) They could envisage their workload better and could plan their work accordingly.

Also during the interviews many staff members commented that the mothers appeared to treat them differently—they appeared more friendly. The analysis of responses to some of the open-ended questions suggested that 'contact with the patients' was an important factor in the satisfaction of the nurses/midwives with their jobs. Yet the questionnaire analysis showed that there was little difference in this area between the wards and in the pre- and post-change periods. Were the nursing staff experiencing changes which in fact did not exist? Was a 'Hawthorne effect' generated by the excitement of being involved in a pioneering new venture? Unfortunately, it is not possible to say. However, if the results are taken at face value, that is the nursing staff appeared to like the system of patient allocation although there was little change in job satisfaction, then three possible explanations for these results can be suggested.

1. It is possible that although the nursing staff like the system of patient allocation, their assessment of job satisfaction depends more upon other factors. Contrary to popular nursing belief, the method used to organise the delivery of care, may only have a relatively minor influence on a particular nurse or midwife's assessment of her job satisfaction. Wallis and Cope (1980) have pointed out that the principles of job redesign have emerged mainly from studies of manufacturing industry and claim that it is hazardous to generalise from them to skilled and professional environments. They suggested that improvements in quality of working life and job satisfaction for nurses may be contingent upon other factors in the work situation which have not hitherto figured so prominently in the literature.

2. It is possible that a system of patient allocation may *change* the nature of the nurse patient relationship and factors such as responsibility and decision making, without necessarily *improving* them.

The interviews with the nursing staff suggested that the changes made little difference to the amount of responsibility experienced by the more senior staff. Nurses and midwives in training are given more responsibility as they gain in experience regardless of the method used to organise the delivery of care. Similarly, one of the pupil midwives interviewed stated that on the 'control' ward the staff knew a little about all the patients whereas on the 'research' and 'pilot' wards they knew a lot about a few patients. Each system she felt, had its advantages. Thus a change to a system of patient allocation may only involve a *different* kind of responsibility, a *different* kind of decision making, and a *different* kind of relationship with the patients.

3. It is possible that the lack of differences in the pre- and post-change measurements of job satisfaction on the wards where the system of patient allocation was introduced may have been because the nursing staff had 'adjusted' to a new level of job satisfaction and the questionnaire was not sensitive enough to measure changes in 'adjustment'.

A final point to consider is that if job satisfaction is already quite high, as it was in this study in all the wards in the pre-change period—is it reasonable to expect it to go higher? Would a finely calibrated response scale on a questionnaire provide any information which was either meaningful or useful? It is possible that the fact that job satisfaction was high on the 'research' ward and the 'pilot' ward was one reason why the changes were accepted. The fact that morale on both wards was good, that the staff enjoyed their work and were concerned for their patients may have been why the changes were implemented with a reasonable degree of success despite the upheavals and problems which accompanied them.

FIGURE 4
Diagram of the Reformulated Conceptual Framework

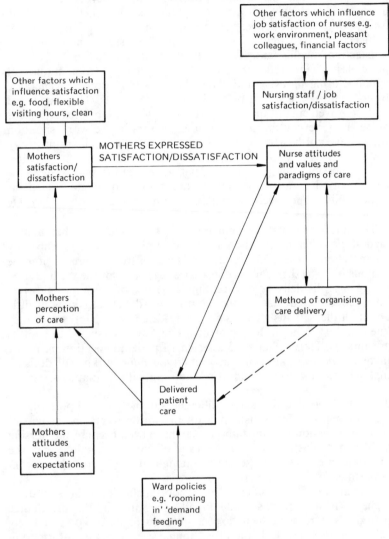

8.3 Reformulation of the Conceptual Framework

The main conclusion to be drawn from this study was that although the nursing staff did express a preference for the new system of work, it made little difference to the mothers expressed satisfaction with care. Thus the results obtained in this study are basically, similar to those obtained by Auld (1968), Chavasse (1978) and Boekholdt and

Kanters (1978) and provide little evidence to support the *reputed* advantages to patients of a system of patient allocation. However, additionally, this study did answer some of the limitations inherent in the methodologies of the previous studies.

Although all the studies had limitations in their research design, methods and instruments used, the fact that four similar studies each using different research design methods and instruments to observe and measure effects have all produced essentially similar results make it very likely that the research findings are reliable.

A simple diagrammatic representation of the conceptual framework of the study was given in Figure 1. Figure 4 shows a reformulated conceptual framework which takes into account the findings of this study and which future researchers may find useful when attempting to examine the relationship between the method of organising care delivery and other variables such as patient satisfaction and staff job satisfaction.

The diagram now suggests that:

(a) While the nurses' attitudes, values and paradigms of care are still assumed to affect and be affected by the method of organising care delivery, the relationship between the method of care delivery and delivered patient care is much weaker than had previously been assumed.

(b) Delivered patient care is directly influenced by the attitudes, values and paradigms of care held by the nursing staff regardless of how the delivery is organised. Delivered patient care is also influenced by specific ward policies which again may be independent of the method of organising care delivery. In the case of a maternity ward such policies would be 'rooming in' and 'demand feeding'.

(c) The mothers' satisfaction/dissatisfaction is still affected by her perception of care received but the method of organising the delivery of care has less influence than previously assumed. The mothers satisfaction/dissatisfaction may also be influenced by other factors which may be unrelated to or only indirectly related to the behaviour of the nursing staff, for example, the quality of the food, the cleanliness of the toilets, the flexibility of the visiting arrangements etc.

(d) The job satisfaction of the nursing staff is still influenced by the method of delivering care through its consistency with the attitudes, values and paradigms of care of the nursing staff. But this is now seen as one influence among many others.

8.4 Further Explanations

The findings of the observation study suggested that there were some differences in the pre- and post-change measurements which were likely to have been caused by the introduction of the system of patient allocation. It is possible also that the nature of the nurse patient relationship was changed. However, the changes were not reflected in either improved patient satisfaction or improved job satisfaction of the nursing staff and explanations for this were suggested. The acceptability of these explanations ultimately depends on whether or not the reader considers that the system of patient allocation had been satisfactorily introduced. The re-examination of the observation study data suggested that the nursing staff were only really allocated to patients on shift 1 of the post-change period and although there were aspects of the system which extended beyond these particular shifts, critics could still say of the findings of this study:

"what did you expect? The nurses were not doing it properly. If only you/they had . . . done/said . . ."

The image and the reality

The criticism that the nursing staff were not "doing it properly" certainly has some credibility. However, it is important not to accept it blindly and totally dismiss the findings of the study. Rather, one must examine the criticism in more detail because it has implications for future research studies, particularly those concerned with evaluating the nursing process.

Research into the advantages of patient centred care and the disadvantages of task centred care is complicated by the fact that the image has become confused with the reality. Methods of delivering nursing care such as task allocation and patient allocation are often considered to be observable forms, where in fact it would be more suitable to consider them to be 'ideal types'. A point recognised by Moult *et al.* (1978) and reiterated recently by Webb (1981). Furthermore, not only is it assumed that there is one clearly defined and recognisable method of delivering patient centred care, for example patient allocation, but it is also assumed that what is not patient allocation is task allocation (and thus by definition not 'patient centred'); assumptions also recognised by Moult *et al.* (1978). However, if patient allocation and task allocation are ideal types and not observable organisational forms, then it is not valid to explain away 'non expected' results by suggesting that the new method of organising the delivery of patient care does not match the 'ideal type'.

Metcalf (1982) suggested that patient allocation and task allocation are associated with different paradigms of care. If this is so, then sisters who hold a task centred paradigm would be more likely to organise the delivery of care on their wards using a system of task allocation. Sisters who hold a patient centred paradigm of care would, on the other hand, be more likely to organise their wards using a system of patient allocation. More likely but not invariably. Letters to the press (Higgins, 1978; Buchan, 1978) the work of Moult *et al.*

(1978) and the evidence from this study suggest that distinctions are often blurred. Thus it is theoretically possible to use a system of task allocation yet hold a patient centred paradigm of care or alternatively use a system of patient allocation but hold a task centred paradigm of care (patients being seen as whole sets of tasks). The fact that neither combination is likely to result in an effective method of delivering care does not mean that the combinations cannot exist.

The evidence from this study suggests that while the 'research' ward may never have achieved the stereotyped version of patient allocation and patient centred care, it never actually started from the stereotyped version of task allocation and task centred care. What the change to the system of patient allocation did, was to provide the nursing staff with a structure which made it easier for them to give a more patient centred form of care. Whether the patient centred care was then given depended on a number of factors,one of the most important of which was the attitude and training of the particular nurse or midwife.

8.5 Implications for Future Research

The theoretical, methodological and practical implications of the results of the study will now be discussed.

(a) *Theoretical Implications*

The theoretical basis of the reputed advantages of a system of patient allocation had its roots in the assumption that the desired care outcomes could be achieved by manipulating task and structural variables. However, underlying this theoretical basis were two further assumptions.

(i) That all nurses respect the importance of the individual needs of patients and the importance of the psychosocial aspects of illness.
(ii) That the nature of the nurse patient relationship is an important determinant of patient care and patient satisfaction.

If these relationships are not actually true, for all nurses and for all relationships, then it is unlikely that the manipulation of task and structural variables will result in the prescribed outcomes. The findings of the patient observation study suggested that the total amount of contact that an individual mother had with the nursing staff during the periods observed, was comparatively short (Table 7). Mothers had much more contact with the other mothers and probably their visitors. Relationships between hospital staff and patients clearly matter, but in the transitory care of the maternity ward, the primary relationship is mother–foetus to mother–child, then followed by mother–mother and mother–nurse/doctor.

However, even if the above mentioned assumptions are true, given the limitations on the effectiveness of manipulating structural variables documented elsewhere (Scottish National Nursing and Midwifery Committee, 1976; Evers, 1982) then it is still open to question whether the desired outcomes would have been achieved and demonstrated in this study. Achieving such outcomes would involve changes in the attitude of staff and patients as well as changes in professional norms—all of which take time. In this respect the time required to change from a task centred paradigm of care is similar to that for any other change in social values. The evidence from this study, suggesting that the paradigms of care held by the nurses and midwives both before and after the change, fell somewhere in between the ideal types of task-centred and patient centred paradigms described above, supports the view that a change of this type should be seen as a process, or at least part of a process, and not as a fixed and wholly definable event.

The evidence from this study was that apart from the general goodwill and dedication of the nursing staff there was no particular change in the nurse-patient relationships. This might have been because of the very short time in which the patients were in the wards; it might also have been because of the lack of capacity in managing the nurse-patient relationship which both the nurses and mothers shared.

If a change from a task-centred paradigm of care to a patient-centred paradigm of care is to be seen as a process rather than an event then a more appropriate method of examining the 'change' might be to adopt an approach such as that outlined by Benson (1977). Benson advocated a dialectic approach to the study of organisations and organisational structures, because it places the processes through which organisational arrangements are produced and maintained at the centre of analysis. Thus it allows for the interplay between social structure and ongoing social construction. Using this approach it would be possible:

(i) to examine the effects that a change in the method of organising the delivery of care might have on the existing organisational structure at different periods of time;
(ii) to assess what changes in the structure could be realised, where obstacles lay, and what powerful groups it would be necessary to align with in order to achieve these changes.

Such an approach would link changes in the methods of organising the delivery of care to changes in, and ideas about, structural and social arrangements which exist in the larger society. It might also help to explain why, over the past 30 or so years, some attempts to introduce methods of organising the delivery of nursing care consistent with a patient centred paradigm of care, have failed, or at least not lasted very long, while others have succeeded and survived.

Dean and Bolton (1980) argued that the specific nature of nursing is extricably linked to prevailing ideas about health, sickness and social structure. They suggested that nursing cannot be considered to be external to the techniques and agencies of the forms of power which constitute the administrative machinery. Consequently the moves to support the delivery of nursing care, by methods consistent with a patient centred paradigm of care, should be viewed in the context of the prevailing movement for a Health Service geared to be more responsive to the needs of the patient as reflected in recent Government publications such as 'Patients First' (DHSS, 1979) and the Second Report of the Social Services Committee (Short), (DHSS, 1980).

A central puzzle in all of the studies on moves to patient-centred care, including moves towards the nursing process, is the degree to which the patient, him or herself, is the active or passive recipient of care. De La Questa (1983) described how the concept of 'patient involvement' in the British nursing context (as opposed to the American nursing context) meant gaining the co-operation and collaboration of the patient rather than involving him or her in active participation in decision making. However, if nursing care is to be individualised to meet the needs of individual patients then the next conceptual step must be to involve the patients in their own treatment for they are in the best position to know what their needs are. This ideal of active patient involvement is only revolutionary in relation to physical medicine for it has been an element of psychotherapeutic care for many years.

(b) *Methodological Implications*

If a change from a task centred paradigm of care to a patient centred paradigm of care is to be considered as a process and not an event, then an experimental approach is not a suitable method of assessing outcomes or advantages. In addition, the use of terms such as task allocation, patient allocation (and nursing process), even as ideal types, should be avoided because they evoke stereotyped and static conceptions of nurses and nursing and thus cause the image to be confused with the reality. The findings of this study suggested that the system of patient allocation which was introduced made little difference to patient satisfaction. This does not mean that the changes in the method of organising the delivery of nursing care had no effect upon any patient outcomes. It may be that the introduction of a system of patient care affects other variables which have hitherto been unexamined. Recent work by Miller (1984) supports this suggestion. Miller found that in her study of elderly patients in geriatric wards, patients who had been in nursing process wards for more than a month, were less incontinent, less dependent and very much happier than similar patients in task allocation wards. These changes were not evident in patients who had been in either type of ward for less than a month.

If the aim of future research is to assess the advantages of using a patient centred method of delivering care then it is important to develop a scheme for measuring the 'quality' of delivered care. How the 'quality' of delivered nursing care can be measured is the subject of much discussion among nurse managers and nurse researchers. The evidence from this study and others (for example, Perkins, 1978) suggests that assessing patient satisfaction with care may not be the most suitable means of assessing the 'quality' of that care because the assessment of patient satisfaction with care is itself bedevilled by a number of pitfalls. This does not mean that the views of the patient are unimportant or irrelevant. Instruments used to measure the 'quality' of nursing care must, if they are to be practical, take account of the views of those who will be affected by them. This includes patients, nurses and doctors.

(c) *Practical Implications*

Apart from the theoretical and methodological implications of the results of the study, there are practical implications which should be of interest to those who are responsible for organising the delivery of nursing care and who wish to change their method of organising the delivery of nursing care so that it is more consistent with a patient centred approach.

(1) *The method by which patient centred care should be delivered*

Controversy exists among nurses about the precise nature of the organisational details and nurse deployment patterns which are necessary to deliver patient centred care. For example, should nurses be allocated to one patient or a group of patients? Can a group of nurses care for a group of patients? How much responsibility should junior nurses be given? To whom, and for what are they accountable?

The results of this study suggest that what is needed is not a 'blueprint' or 'ideal type' but a recognition that the organisation of the delivery of care has to be contingent upon a number of factors. For example, the nature of the patient's condition, and the workload that this generates; the quality and quantity of the available nursing staff and hours that they can work; the expectations of the patients; the expectations of the other hospital staff who have business on the ward; the educational needs of the nursing staff in training. The degree of patient-centredness of delivered care depends on more than external manifestations. Thus the method by which patient centred care should be delivered is, at any given time, determined by the resources available and the nature of the patient's condition.

(2) *Communication*

In this study the nurses and midwives interviewed said that when they used a system of patient allocation, they knew more about the patients. There was evidence in the study to suggest that the ward reports were longer, and contained more information. Some of the nurses and midwives commented that because they had fewer patients to concentrate on, the information they did receive meant more to them. The way that nurses communicate, or rather do not communicate, with patients, is an area to which considerable research time has been devoted (Faulkner, 1979; Macilwaine, 1980; Clarke, 1981). The results of such studies suggest that nurses lack communication skills. While this may be true, recent work by Melia (1981) suggests that many nurses, especially junior nurses are deprived of the information they need to be able to communicate effectively. In which case, no matter how many communication skills a nurse has, unless she is given the information she needs, she is not going to be able to use her skills. In this study the system of patient allocation which was introduced appeared to improve communication (at least as far as the nurses and midwives were concerned) because:

(1) the nurses and midwives spent more time in the ward report and were given more information;
(2) the nurses and midwives had fewer patients to concentrate upon.

Individualised Care

In this study both mothers and midwives were asked to explain what they meant by 'individualised care' (see Chapter 4). Although there was some overlapping of explanations the mothers and nursing staff tended to emphasise different areas.

The nurses and midwives tended to emphasise the necessity of care being planned to suit the individual needs of patients with all care, or at least as much as possible, being given by one nurse or midwife. The mothers, on the other hand, tended to emphasise what Luker (1980) called the 'microprocesses of care', that is, the pleasant friendly nurse who remembered to call the mother by her name and did not try to 'fob' her off when she had a problem. When they did have problems, the majority of mothers did not appear to care about how many different members of the nursing staff tried to help, as long as each person knew about the problem and was up to date with the care and advice she had already received. Thus, for a mother, being cared for by pleasant and friendly nurses and midwives who communicate well with each other, is just as likely to make her feel she is being treated as an 'individual', as is receiving all her care from the same nurse or midwife.

Continuity of Care

The development of a good nurse-patient relationship plays an important part in the imagery of nursing and midwifery. Continuity of care is an important element in the development of this relationship, with one nurse/one patient being seen as the 'ideal'. In hospital maternity care, the *lack* of continuity of care has been constantly criticised (Hale, 1985). Unfortunately, the realities of hospital life put constraints upon the extent to which the ideal of continuity of care can be realistically achieved. Although it was suggested above that for the patients, 'individualised care' did not necessarily necessitate 'continuity of care', the majority of mothers did enjoy having the same nurses and midwives coming back to care for them.

Because nurses and midwives are not on duty all day, and every day, perfect continuity of care for hospital patients is an unrealistic ideal. However, as was demonstrated in this study, improvements in continuity of care can be made, and although they were small, they were appreciated by the patients. Nevertheless, when planning improvements in the continuity of care, it is important to remember, that too much continuity of care in a hospital ward which contains a variety of personnel with different levels of skill and experience, could possibly result in *poorer* care. Patients have a right to be cared for by skilled personnel. On the other hand, less skilled personnel have to gain experience. If patients have contact with skilled personnel potential problems are likely to be noticed early. But, if the patients only see less skilled personnel, these potential problems may remain unnoticed until they become real, and perhaps serious problems.

Part-time Staff

When care is delivered by allocating nurses to patients, it should be possible to accommodate part-time staff. Problems can arise, however, when the part-time staff member is a senior nurse who would previously have been expected to be 'in charge' when she was on duty. The extent of the possible problems depend upon how 'part-time' the staff member is. Some part-time staff in hospitals work only a few hours less than full-time staff members, others work only a few hours each week. If a part-time staff member is on duty some part of most days, problems are less likely to emerge. However, if the part-time staff member only works a few hours, one or two days a week, some problems may emerge, and if the particular staff member is a senior grade, problems may less easily be resolved. Staff members who only work a few hours each week are less likely to have amassed the background information that most nurses acquire after being on duty for a few days. This can put a senior part-time staff member at a disadvantage if she is left in charge when a system of patient allocation is being used, because she is likely to have less knowledge about the particular patients than the junior staff. Moreover, it may be difficult for her to acquire the necessary information quickly.

Although the reaction of part-time staff will depend to some extent upon their own personality and attitudes, if the method by which nurses organise themselves to deliver care is being re-organised, then it is important to be fully aware of the problems which may face part-time staff, to involve them fully in pre-change discussions and make arrangements so that their problems can be minimised.

Functional Staff

The organisation of the delivery of patient care using a system whereby nurses are allocated to patients is easier when available staff can perform a whole range of nursing duties. Problems can arise when some members of staff can, or expect to perform only certain duties. In this study the person most affected by this problem was the nursery nurse, but similar problems could occur with other staff in different areas. Because the nursery nurse felt that she was employed to look after babies—all of them, not just some of them, she took exception to being 'expected' to help with the general care of the mothers.

Nursery nurses were originally introduced into maternity wards to compensate for the shortage of trained midwives and pupil midwives. Because their area of expertise was babies, and because the ward work was so organised that the care of the mothers and babies was technically separate, they could make a useful and valuable contribution. However, when the care of the mothers and babies is no longer functionally divided, what is the role of the nursery nurse? Given the perennial shortages of qualified and pupil midwives, should the role of the nursery nurse be developed so that she becomes involved with the more general care of the mother? Or should she be replaced by a general purpose maternity worker with more training than an auxiliary but less than a qualified midwife—similar perhaps to a State Enrolled Nurse.

A recent report on the future of nursery nursing (NNEB, 1981) paid little attention to the future problems facing the employment of nursery nurses in post-natal wards. They did not appear to be aware of the existence of any trends in nursing or midwifery which might affect the role of the nursery nurse, or if they were aware they did not mention them. Neither did the professional nursing and midwifery organisations which gave evidence appear to consider these trends worth mentioning. The Royal College of Midwives, while endorsing the employment of nursery nurses in post-natal wards (provided that further training was given to equip the nursery nurses with the necessary skills) gave little advice about the content of the further

Example of Data Collection Sheet for Nursing Staff Observation Study

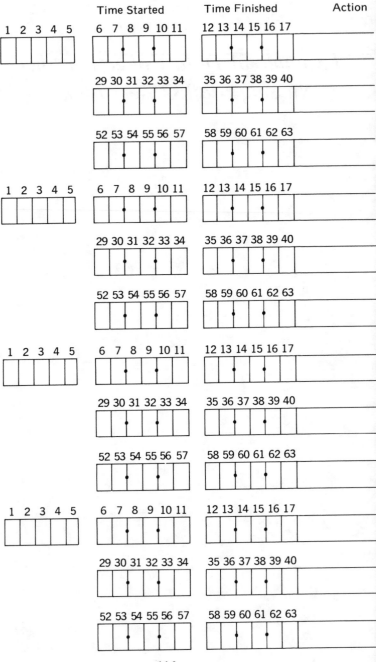

Time Started   Time Finished   Action

	A/N M B	Involving	Initiator	Initiating Factor	Other Nurses	Other
18 19 20	21	22 23 24	25	26	27	28
41 42 43	44	45 46 47	48	49	50	51
64 65 66	67	68 69 70	71	72	73	74
18 19 20	21	22 23 24	25	26	27	28
41 42 43	44	45 46 47	48	49	50	51
64 65 66	67	68 69 70	71	72	73	74
18 19 20	21	22 23 24	25	26	27	28
41 42 43	44	45 46 47	48	49	50	51
64 65 66	67	68 69 70	71	72	73	74
18 19 20	21	22 23 24	25	26	27	28
41 42 43	44	45 46 47	48	49	50	51
64 65 66	67	68 69 70	71	72	73	74

117

Example of the Code List for the Nursing Staff Observation Study

BASIC

This category includes any kind of activity which could be carried out by personnel with no formal midwifery or nursing training, or by student nurses on secondment, without supervision by trained midwifery staff.

Code
001 Stripping and making beds
002 Tidying beds, including making patients comfortable
003 Bedbathing patients, washing in bed, including remaking beds
004 Supervising patients in bathroom/showers
005 Escorting to and from bathroom/showers
006 Care of pressure areas
007 Giving, taking, emptying bedpan/commode
008 Providing facilities for washing hands after using bedpan/commode
009 Testing urine
010 Assisting patients getting up including assisting to toilet
011 Filling fluid balance charts
012 Helping lift patient on/off trolley
013 Escorting patients to and from department (inc. escorting to front lodge) inc. time in department
014 In bathroom, sluice or kitchen, activity unidentified
015 General care of mouth, hair or nails
016 Giving patients food or drink
017 Preparing cot for baby
018 Feeding baby
019 'Top and tailing' baby
020 Changing baby's nappy
021 Tidying and/or cleaning equipment or working area
022 Stocking up lockers or cupboards
023 Escorting baby to and from somewhere
024 Making baby comfortable in cot
025 Answering patient's call bell
026 Preparing bottle feeds
027 Preparing working area for procedure (Miscellaneous)
028 Moving beds
029 Cuddling baby, comforting crying baby
030 Preparing bed for new admission (uncomplicated)
031 Checking a chart, e.g. fluid chart or feed chart which is at *patient's bedside*
032 Chaperoning a doctor

Initiating Factor Categories

A. Clinical	(a)	nurse performs some procedure on mother or baby
	(b)	nurse goes to inform mother of some impending procedure
	(c)	gives drugs
	(d)	fills in charts
B. Clinical	(a)	mother reports something about herself or her baby to the nurse
C. Surveillance	(a)	nurse checks that mother is OK
	(b)	nurse checks that mother is performing some procedure adequately without supervision
	(c)	nurse checks that mother has had something done that she was supposed to have had done
D. Information	(a)	nurse asks mother for information
	(b)	nurse gives mother information
	(c)	mother asks nurse for information
E. Education	(a)	nurse teaches patient something (involving equipment or action)
	(b)	nurse gives mother advice
	(c)	nurse gives mother some clinical knowledge about childbirth and/or babies etc.
F. Advice	(a)	mother asks nurse for help and/or advice
G. Social conversation	(a)	nurse chats to mother
	(b)	mother chats to nurse
H. Emotional support	(a)	nurse goes to comfort a distressed mother
I. Baby	(a)	nurse makes some social interaction with baby
	(b)	nurse makes a comment (not clinical) about baby to mother
	(c)	nurse takes baby to mother
	(d)	nurse cuddles baby to comfort it
	(g)	baby cries
J. Equipment	(a)	nurse gives something to mother
	(b)	mother asks nurse for something e.g.: linen/telephone/bed pan/bottle
	(c)	mother gives something to nurse
K. Housekeeping	(a)	nurse goes to make beds, clean/tidy rooms etc.

APPENDIX D

Codes for Grades of Nursing Staff

Sister	8
Staff midwife	7
Senior pupil midwife	6
Junior pupil	5
B.-Nurse (university)	4
Ob. Nurse	3
Nursery Nurse	2
Auxiliary	1

Example of Data Collection Sheet for Patient Observation Study

1 2 3 4 5	6 7 8 9 10 11	12 13 14 15 16 17
	25 26 27 28 29 30	31 32 33 34 35 36
	44 45 46 47 48 49	50 51 52 53 54 55

1 2 3 4 5	6 7 8 9 10 11	12 13 14 15 16 17
	25 26 27 28 29 30	31 32 33 34 35 36
	44 45 46 47 48 49	50 51 52 53 54 55

1 2 3 4 5	6 7 8 9 10 11	12 13 14 15 16 17
	25 26 27 28 29 30	31 32 33 34 35 36
	44 45 46 47 48 49	50 51 52 53 54 55

1 2 3 4 5	6 7 8 9 10 11	12 13 14 15 16 17
	25 26 27 28 29 30	31 32 33 34 35 36
	44 45 46 47 48 49	50 51 52 53 54 55

1 2 3 4 5	6 7 8 9 10 11	12 13 14 15 16 17
	25 26 27 28 29 30	31 32 33 34 35 36
	44 45 46 47 48 49	50 51 52 53 54 55

...ction   Nurse Interaction   Baby Interaction
                                Initia.

                        Nurse   Factor Initiator
18 19   20 21   22   23   24
☐☐   ☐☐   ☐   ☐   ☐

37 38   39 40   41   42   43
☐☐   ☐☐   ☐   ☐   ☐

56 57   58 59   60   61   62
☐☐   ☐☐   ☐   ☐   ☐

18 19   20 21   22   23   24
☐☐   ☐☐   ☐   ☐   ☐

37 38   39 40   41   42   43
☐☐   ☐☐   ☐   ☐   ☐

56 57   58 59   60   61   62
☐☐   ☐☐   ☐   ☐   ☐

18 19   20 21   22   23   24
☐☐   ☐☐   ☐   ☐   ☐

37 38   39 40   41   42   43
☐☐   ☐☐   ☐   ☐   ☐

56 57   58 59   60   61   62
☐☐   ☐☐   ☐   ☐   ☐

18 19   20 21   22   23   24
☐☐   ☐☐   ☐   ☐   ☐

37 38   39 40   41   42   43
☐☐   ☐☐   ☐   ☐   ☐

56 57   58 59   60   61   62
☐☐   ☐☐   ☐   ☐   ☐

18 19   20 21   22   23   24
☐☐   ☐☐   ☐   ☐   ☐

37 38   39 40   41   42   43
☐☐   ☐☐   ☐   ☐   ☐

56 57   58 59   60   61   62
☐☐   ☐☐   ☐   ☐   ☐

Rules for Observation for the Nursing Staff Observation Study

1. When nurse is alone indicate activity category.
2. When nurse is with patient but performing a procedure indicate activity category. If it involves interaction with a patient, indicate patient and initiating factor.
3. When a nurse is performing a procedure such as feeding a baby, and different mothers come up and interact with her, then each interaction is listed separately from the total time that the procedure takes. This means that the nurse will be recorded as doing two things at the same time. *Do not* enter these interactions with patients as social conversation.
4. Interactions with mothers are only recorded as (407) when *no* clinical work is going on. If the nurse subsequently starts to perform an activity then code it as a new activity.
5. When nurse interacts with more than one mother simultaneously, then list the mothers in separate columns.
6. Try to have the nurses activities following on continuously.
7. When the nurse is accompanying a doctor on a ward round, do not list interactions with individual patients, but only the total time engaged in the activity.
   (Reason—the nurse is not the prime interactor in this situation. However if another nurse or patient interrupts the nurse on the ward round and asks her a specific question, then record the interaction separately.)
8. If a nurse is performing a procedure but talking to another nurse, indicate presence of the other nurse.
9. (a) When a nurse goes into a room and addresses a group of patients she is interacting with all of them.
   (b) If a nurse goes into a room, does not say anything to the group of patients, but then either goes to talk to one mother, or carries out some task e.g. bedmaking—record the latter interaction or activity.
   (c) If the nurse goes into a room, addresses no-one, but starts, e.g. to make beds, then interaction only starts when one or more mothers attract her attention.
10. When nurse is preparing to give drugs or do obs. eg: collecting equipment code under activity e.g.: giving drugs—103.

Rules for Observation for the Patient Observation Study

1. Do not record all mother activities, only those which have been pre-coded.
2. Do not record interactions between mother and other patients.
3. If mother is interacting with baby, e.g.: feeding, record any interactions with nurses that occur during this period. Thus mothers may be doing more than one activity at the same time.
4. If a nurse walks into the room and addresses all the mothers, then interaction between nurse and observed mother starts. It stops when the nurse is no longer receptive to replies i.e.: if the nurse turns to another patient or engrosses herself in another task.

The Expectation Questionnaire (Main Study)

University of Manchester
Department of Nursing

May 1979

This questionnaire is part of a project being carried out by a Research Associate of Manchester University Department of Nursing. The project is being funded by the Department of Health and Social Security.

The aim of the project is to find out what mothers-to-be expect it to be like in hospital after they have had their baby.

Your participation in this study will be greatly appreciated. All replies are completely confidential and will only be seen by the research worker.

Code No....... Questionnaire

The following questionnaire is designed to find out what YOU expect it to be like in hospital after you have had your baby. Below, you will find a number of statements describing the expectations that some mothers-to-be have about their forthcoming stay in hospital. Can you indicate what YOU think your stay in hospital might be like by ticking the appropriate category after the statement.

1. I expect that the nurses in hospital will teach me how to bath and feed my baby.

   Definitely yes ....
   Quite likely ....
   Don't know ....
   Unlikely ....
   Definitely not ....

2. I expect that the nurses in hospital will be too busy to deal with any problems that I might have.

   Definitely yes ....
   Quite likely ....
   Don't know ....
   Unlikely ....
   Definitely not ....

3. I expect that I will be able to feed my baby whenever I think it is hungry.

      Definitely yes   ....
      Quite likely   ....
      Don't know   ....
      Unlikely   ....
      Definitely not   ....

4. I expect that I will only be able to have my baby with me when he/she needs to be fed, changed or bathed.

      Definitely yes   ....
      Quite likely   ....
      Don't know   ....
      Unlikely   ....
      Definitely not   ....

5. I expect that in the ward, after I have had the baby I will be looked after by one or two particular nurses.

      Definitely yes   ....
      Quite likely   ....
      Don't know   ....
      Unlikely   ....
      Definitely not   ....

6. I expect that if I have any problems or worries I will be able to ask the nurses for help.

      Definitely yes   ....
      Quite likely   ....
      Don't know   ....
      Unlikely   ....
      Definitely not   ....

7. I expect that I will be able to have my baby at my bedside all the time.

      Definitely yes   ....
      Quite likely   ....
      Don't know   ....
      Unlikely   ....
      Definitely not   ....

8. I expect that the nurses will come round and ask me if I am having any problems.

      Definitely yes   ....
      Quite likely   ....
      Don't know   ....
      Unlikely   ....
      Definitely not   ....

9. I expect that I will have to feed my baby at set times, e.g.: every four hours.

Definitely yes	....
Quite likely	....
Don't know	....
Unlikely	....
Definitely not	....

10. I expect that in the ward, after I have had the baby, I will be looked after by a lot of different nurses.

Definitely yes	....
Quite likely	....
Don't know	....
Unlikely	....
Definitely not	....

11. I expect that the nurses will be too busy to come round and ask me if I am having any problems.

Definitely yes	....
Quite likely	....
Don't know	....
Unlikely	....
Definitely not	....

12. I expect that the nurses in hospital will be too busy to teach me how to bath and feed my baby myself.

Definitely yes	....
Quite likely	....
Don't know	....
Unlikely	....
Definitely not	....

Before you return the questionnaire can you please answer the questions on the next page.

Sample Variables

1 How many children do you have?..

2. Did you have any in this hospital?...

3. Have you been in hospital before? ....
(apart from having babies)

4. Have you been going to:
(a) Parentcraft or mothercraft classes..
(b) Relaxation classes...

5. Have you been visited at home by the midwife?...

6. Have you been shown:
   (a) The room where you will have the baby?...
   (b) The ward where you will be after you have had the baby?...................

Q13. Some people dread going in to hospital to have a baby. Are YOU expecting it to be an enjoyable experience?...
   (Can you give me a reason for your answer?)

   ....

   ....

   ....

The Job Satisfaction Questionnaire (Main Study)

Department of Nursing
University of Manchester
Stopford Building
Oxford Road
Manchester M13 9PT

September 1979

This questionnaire is part of a research project being carried out by myself, Claire Metcalf, a nursing research fellow at Manchester University. The project is being funded by the Department of Health and Social Security, and is being supervised by the University Department of Nursing.

The purpose of the questionnaire is to find out what nurses and midwives like and dislike about their work and how they would like to see it improved. There are no right or wrong answers, the best answer is your personal opinion.

Each questionnaire is completely anonymous. The only information you are asked to give is your ward, grade, qualifications and years of experience. This will help me to find out if people of different grades and experience have different points of view, and different problems.

The completed questionnaires will be treated confidentially. No one will see them except myself. I will collect them from you on the ward and immediately remove them to the University.

Most of the questions only require you to tick one of a few possible answers. A few require you to tick more than one answer, but these questions are clearly indicated. Some questions require you to write a sentence or two to give me a little more information. These questions are important and will assist me in understanding what you like and dislike about your job—please do not omit them. Finally, if you would care to write any other comments about your work you are very welcome.

I do hope you will help me. Please ask me if you have any problems completing the questionnaire and if you wish any further information.

Yours sincerely,
Claire A. Metcalf

Grade ....

Years Qualified ....
(For auxiliaries—number of years as an auxiliary)

130

Qualifications ....

7	8	9	10

11	12	13	14

15	16	17	18

QUESTION 1:

A. How often during your working day is your work fairly routine?
   (1) Always   ....
   (2) Often   ....
   (3) About half the time   ....
   (4) Occasionally   ....
   (5) Rarely   ....

19 ☐

B. If you ticked 1, 2 or 3—is it *routine* because?
   (Please tick as many as apply to your job)
   (1) There are very few problems for you to solve   ....
   (2) You do the same set of tasks all day every day   ....
   (3) You have very little responsibility
   (4) The work requires very little skill and knowledge
   ....

If it is routine for any other reason, please write the reason below:

20 ☐
21 ☐
22 ☐
23 ☐

24	25

C. Is the amount of routine in your job?
   (1) Too much   ....
   (2) Too little   ....
   (3) About right   ....

26 ☐

QUESTION 2:

A. How often during your working day do you feel that your job is a real challenge to your ability?
   (1) Always   ....
   (2) Often   ....
   (3) About half the time   ....
   (4) Occasionally   ....
   (5) Never   ....

27 ☐
28 ☐

B. If you have ticked 1, 2 or 3—is it challenging because?
   (Please tick as many as apply to your job)
   (1) You have difficult problems to solve   ....
   (2) You have a number of very different kinds of tasks to perform   ....
   (3) You have a great deal of responsibility   ....
   (4) The work requires special skills and knowledge, which you have   ....

29 ☐
30 ☐
31 ☐

131

If it is challenging for any other reason, please write reason below:

....

....

....

32 33

C. Is the amount of challenge in your job?
    (1) Too much   34
    (2) Too little   ....
    (3) About right   ....

QUESTION 3:

A. How often do you get a sense of achievement from your work?
    (1) Almost every day   ....
    (2) About once a week   35
    (3) About once every few weeks   ....
    (4) Less than once a month   ....
    (5) Hardly ever   ....

B. What gives you most sense of achievement in work?

....

....   36

....

....

C. Would you like to get a sense of achievement?
    (1) More often   37
    (2) About the same as at present   ....
    (3) It doesn't matter to me   ....
    If you answered (1) to question 3C—what would give *you* more sense of achievement at work?

D. ....

....   38 39

....

....

QUESTION 4:

A. How well do you think your skills and knowledge are used in your present job?
    (1) Very well used   ....
    (2) Quite well used   40
    (3) Sometimes well used, sometimes not   ....
    (4) Poorly used   ....
    (5) Very poorly used   ....
    If you have ticked 1, 2 or 3 to question 4A—about what amount of your time at work are your skills and knowledge well used?

B. (1) Almost all the time ....
   (2) About three-quarters of the time ....
   (3) About one-quarter of the time ....
   (4) Less than one-quarter of the time ....

   41 □

If you have ticked 3, 4 or 5 to question 4A—would you state below why you think your skills and knowledge are not being well used in your present job:

C. ....
   ....
   ....
   ....

   42 43 □□

What do you think are your own particular skills and knowledge?

D. ....
   ....
   ....
   ....

   44 45 □□

E. Would you like there to be better opportunities than there are at present to develop further your skills and knowledge?
   (1) Yes ....
   (2) No ....
   (3) It doesn't matter to me ....

   46 □

QUESTION 5:

A. How much responsibility do you have in your present job?
   (1) A great deal ....
   (2) Quite a lot ....
   (3) A reasonable amount ....
   (4) Very little ....
   (5) None ....

   47 □

B. How much responsibility would you like to have in your job?
   (1) More than now ....
   (2) Less than now ....
   (3) About the same ....

   48 □

QUESTION 6:

A. On most days, when you are working, how often does time seem to drag for you?
   (1) About half a day or more ....
   (2) About one third of the day ....
   (3) About one quarter of the day ....
   (4) Only for small periods ....
   (5) Time never seems to drag ....

   49 □

If you answered 1, 2, 3 or 4 to question 6A—what causes time to drag?

B. 50

....

....

....

QUESTION 7:

Some people are very involved in their work—they practically think and talk of nothing else.
How involved do you feel in your job?
(1) Very little involved, my other interests are more absorbing   ....
(2) Slightly involved   ....
(3) Moderately involved, my job and my other interests are equally absorbing to me   51
(4) Strongly involved   ....
(5) Very strongly involved, my work is the most absorbing interest in my life   ....

QUESTION 8:

When you are given a piece of work to do, how often is it completely up to you to decide how to go about doing it?
(1) Hardly ever   ....
(2) About one-quarter of the time   52
(3) About half the time   ....
(4) About three-quarters of the time   ....
(5) Almost always   ....

QUESTION 9:

A. When you have been given several things to do, how often is it up to you to decide which you will do first and how often are you expected to do things in a set order?
(1) Always expected to do things in a set order   ....
(2) Usually expected to do things in a set order   ....
(3) Sometimes expected to do things in a set order, sometimes up to me to decide which I will do first   53
(4) Usually up to me to decide which I do first   ....
(5) Always up to me to decide which I do first   ....
If you answered 1, 2, 3 or 4 to question 9A—would you answer the question below.

B. If you could choose, would you like to have?
(1) More freedom in choosing the order of work   ....
(2) Prefer to have a stricter order of work   54
(3) Everything is fine at the moment   ....

134

QUESTION 10:

A. In some jobs there are detailed rules about what is the right way to do the job, the correct procedure to adopt. What is it like in your job?
  (1) Almost everything is covered by rules and set procedures ....
  (2) Most things are covered by rules and set procedures .... 55 □
  (3) About half the things are covered by rules and set procedures ....
  (4) There are very few rules and procedures ....
  (5) There are no rules or set procedures for anything ....

B. Would you like to have?
  (1) More rules and procedures than now .... 56 □
  (2) Less rules and procedures than now ....
  (3) About the same ....

QUESTION 11:

A. Would you say that your job provides you with an opportunity to make decisions and use your own judgement?
  (1) Yes—a lot .... 57 □
  (2) Yes—a little ....
  (3) Not at all ....
  If you ticked 1 or 2 to question 11A—what kinds of decisions do you most enjoy taking?
  (Can you give some examples)

B. ....
  ....
  .... 58 59 □□

C. Would you like to have?
  (1) The opportunity to take more decisions than at present .... 60 □
  (2) To make fewer decisions than now ....
  (3) Everything is fine as it is ....

QUESTION 12:

A. If other people who work with you do not do their work efficiently, how often would this create problems for *your* work?
  (1) Almost always ....
  (2) Usually .... 61 □
  (3) About half the time ....
  (4) Occasionally ....
  (5) Very rarely or never ....

135

B. If *you* do not do your own job efficiently, how often would this create problems for your colleagues?
(1) Always ....
(2) Usually 62
(3) About half the time ....
(4) Occasionally ....
(5) Very rarely or never ....

QUESTION 13:

A. If other people you work with do not do their work *fast enough*, how often would this create problems for your work?
(1) Always 63
(2) Usually ....
(3) About half the time ....
(4) Occasionally ....
(5) Very rarely or never ....

B. If *you* do not do your work *fast enough*, how often would this create problems for other people you work with?
(1) Always ....
(2) Usually 64
(3) About half the time ....
(4) Occasionally ....
(5) Very rarely or never ....

QUESTION 14:

Would you prefer to have the kind of job where you are less dependent on the work of others and others are less dependent on your work?
(1) Yes 65
(2) No ....
(3) It makes no difference to me ....

QUESTION 15:

A. Do you always understand what you have to do?
(1) Always understand ....
(2) Understand about 75% of the time 66
(3) Understand about 50% of the time ....
(4) Understand about 25% of the time ....
(5) Hardly ever understand ....

B. Do you always understand *why* you have to do it?
(1) Always understand why ....
(2) Know why about 75% of the time 67
(3) Know why about 50% of the time ....
(4) Know why about 25% of the time ....
(5) Hardly ever know why ....

136

QUESTION 16:

Do you always agree with what you have to do?
(1) Always agree ....
(2) Usually agree ....
(3) Agree about half the time ....
(4) Seldom agree ....
(5) Hardly ever agree ....

68 □

QUESTION 17:

A. How much of your work is checked?
(1) Everything is checked ....
(2) About three-quarters or more is checked ....
(3) About half is checked ....
(4) About a quarter is checked ....
(5) No-one ever checks my work ....

69 □

B. Would you like to have?
(1) Less checking than now ....
(2) More checking than now ....
(3) About the same as at present ....

70 □

QUESTION 18:

A. Do you ever get any feedback from your senior colleagues (e.g.: people like sister, nursing officers, tutors) about how well you are getting on at work?
(1) Regularly ....
(2) Occasionally ....
(3) Never ....
If you answered 2 or 3 to question 18A—please answer question 18B below

71 □

B. Would you like to get more feedback from your senior colleagues?
(1) Yes ....
(2) No ....
(3) It doesn't matter to me ....

72 □

QUESTION 19:

A. Do you ever get the chance to plan the care, or help to plan the care, for a small group of mothers and babies?
(1) Often ....
(2) Occasionally ....
(3) Never ....
If you answered 2 or 3 to question 19A please answer 19B below

73 □

B. Would you like to have the opportunity to do this?
(1) Yes ....
(2) No ....
(3) It doesn't matter to me ....

74 □

QUESTION 20:

A. Do you ever get the chance to look after, or help to look after, a small group of mothers and babies rather than looking after all the mothers or all the babies?
(1) Often ....
(2) Occasionally ....
(3) Never ....
If you answered 3 to question 20A please answer 20C below.

75 ☐

B. Would you like to have the opportunity to do this?
(1) Yes ....
(2) No ....
(3) It doesn't matter to me ....
If you answered 1 or 2 to question 20A please answer 20C below.

76 ☐

C. Do you enjoy working like that?
(1) Yes ....
(2) No ....
(3) It makes no difference to me ....

77 ☐

1	2	3

QUESTION 21:

Taking your job as a whole, how much job satisfaction does it provide you with?
(1) A great deal ....
(2) Quite a lot ....
(3) A moderate amount ....
(4) Very little ....
(5) Hardly any at all ....

4 ☐

QUESTION 22:

Would you tick any of the things in the list below which would increase your job satisfaction.
(If some things make a greater contribution than others please rank these 1, 2, 3, etc.)
(1) The challenge of solving difficult problems ....
(2) Freedom to plan your own work ....
(3) Greater contact with mothers and babies ....
(4) Being responsible for a small group of mothers and babies ....
(5) More use being made of your own skills and knowledge ....

5 ☐
6 ☐
7 ☐
8 ☐
9 ☐

B. Please add anything else which would contribute to your job satisfaction which is not in the list above.
....
....
....
....

QUESTION 23:

What do you like *least* about your work?

10 11

QUESTION 24:

What do you like *most* about your work?

12 13

References

AULD, M. G. (1968). Team nursing in a maternity hospital. *Midwife and Health Visitor,* **4,** pp. 242–245, pp. 302–305.

AULD, M. G. (1976). *How Many Nurses.* Royal College of Nursing, London.

AUSTIN, R. (1978). Professionalism and the nature of nursing reward. *Journal of Advanced Nursing,* **3,** 1, 9–23.

BENSON, J. K. (1977). Organisations: A dialectical view. *Administration Science Quarterly,* **22,** 1–21.

BOEKHOLDT, M. G. and KANTERS, H. W. (1978). Team nursing in a general hospital—theory results and limitations. *Journal of Occupational Psychology,* **51,** 315–325.

BUCHAN, H. (1978). Nursing care. (Letter to the Editor.) *Nursing Times,* **74,** 40, 1643.

CAMERSON, S. (1973). Job satisfaction: The concept and its measurement. *Department of Employment Work Research Units.* Occasional Paper No. 4.

CAMPBELL, D. T. and STANLEY, J. C. (1966). *Experimental and Quasi-Experimental Designs for Research.* Rand McNally Co., Chicago.

CARTWRIGHT, A. (1964). *Human Relations and Hospital Care.* Routledge and Kegan Paul, London.

CARTWRIGHT, A. (1979). *The Dignity of Labour: a Study of Childbearing and Induction.* Tavistock Publications, London.

CHAVASSE, J. (1978). *From Task Assignment to Patient Assignment. A Ward Management Project Evaluated.* Paper presented at the Royal College of Nursing, Research Society Conference, Edinburgh, April. Unpublished. (A paper based on the material presented in this paper has been subsequently published, see Chavasse, 1981.)

CHAVASSE, J. (1981). From task assignment to patient allocation: (a) Change evaluation. *Journal of Advanced Nursing,* **6,** 137–145.

CLARK, J. M. (1981). Communication in nursing. *Nursing Times,* **77,** 1, 12–18.

CLARK, J. and HOCKEY, L. (1979). *Research for Nursing,* HM and M Publishers, Aylesbury, England.

CROW, J. (1977). The nursing process. *Nursing Times,* **73,** 24, 892–896, **73,** 25, 950–957, **73,** 26, 978–982.

DAVIS, F. (1977). 'The Nursing Process', Letter to the Editor. *Nursing Times,* **73,** 29, 1125.

DEAN, M. and BOLTON, G. (1980). The Administration of Poverty and the Development of Nursing Practice in 19th Century England. In: *Rewriting Nursing History.* Davis, C. (Ed.), Croom Helm, London.

DE LA CUESTA, C. (1983). The Nursing process: from development to implementation. *Journal of Advanced Nursing,* **8,** 365–371.

DENZIN, N. K. (1970). *Sociological Methods: A Source Book.* Butterworths, London.

140

DEPARTMENT OF HEALTH AND SOCIAL SECURITY (DHSS). (1979). *Patients First*. Consultative Paper in the Structure and Management of the National Health Service in England and Wales. HMSO, London.

DEPARTMENT OF HEALTH AND SOCIAL SECURITY (DHSS). (1980). *Perinatal and Neonatal Mortality: Second Report of the Social Services Committee (Short)*. HMSO, London.

EVERLY, G. S. and FALCIONE, R. L. (1976). Perceived dimensions of job satisfaction for State Registered Nurses. *Nursing Research,* **25,** 5, 346–348.

EVERS, H. (1982). Key issues in nursing practice: Ward management. *Nursing Times,* Occasional Papers 78, 6, 21–24.

FAULKNER, A. (1979). Monitoring nurse-patient conversations in a ward. *Nursing Times,* Occasional Paper 75, 23, 95–96.

GENERAL NURSING COUNCIL (GNC). (1977). *Educational Policy.* Circular 77/19.

GREENWOOD, J. (1984). Nursing research: a position paper. *Journal of Advanced Nursing,* **9,** 77–82.

HALE, C. (1985). Mothers on the assembly line. *Nursing Mirror,* **161,** No. 6, August 7.

HALL, D., PILL, R. and CLOUGH, F. (1976). Notes for a Conceptual Model of Hospital Experience as an Interactive Process. In: *The Sociology of the National Health Service,* Stacey, M. (Ed.) Sociological Review, Monograph 22, University of Keele.

HERZBERG, F. (1966). The Motivation—Hygiene Theory. In: *Organisation Theory.* Pugh, D. (Ed.). Penguin, London.

HIGGINS, P. (1978). Task versus patient allocation. (Letter to the Editor). *Nursing Times,* **74,** 12, 498.

HOCKEY, L. (1976). *Women in Nursing: A Descriptive Study.* Hodder & Stoughton, London.

JENKINSON, V. (1958). Group or team nursing: report on a five-year experiment at St. Georges Hospital, London. *Nursing Times,* **54,** 3, 62–64, **54,** 4, 92–93.

JENKINSON, V. (1961). Team nursing. *Nursing Times,* **57,** 9, 264–266.

KITZINGER, S. (1979). *The Good Birth Guide.* Fontana Paperbacks, London.

LUKER, K. A. (1980). *Health Visiting and the Elderly: An Experimental Study to Evaluate the Effects of Focussed Health Visitor Intervention on Elderly Women Living Alone at Home.* Unpublished Ph.D Thesis, University of Edinburgh.

MACILWAINE, H. (1980). *The Nursing of - Female Neurotic Patients in Psychiatric Units of General Hospitals.* Unpublished Ph.D Thesis, Manchester University.

MARKS-MARAN, D. (1978). Patient allocation v. task allocation in relation to the nursing process. *Nursing Times,* **74,** 10, 413–416.

MATHEWS, A. (1972). Total patient care in the ward. *Nursing Mirror,* **134,** 6, 29–31.

MCKENNEL, A. (1974). *Surveying Attitude Structures: A Discussion of Principles and Procedures.* Elsevier, Amsterdam.

MELIA, K. (1981). *Student Nurses' Accounts of their Work and Training: A Qualitative Analysis.* Unpublished Ph.D Thesis, University of Edinburgh.

MENZIES, I. (1960). A case study on the functioning of social systems as a defense against anxiety. *Human Relations,* **13,** 95–121.

141

METCALF, C. A. (1982). *A Study of a Change in The Method of Organising the Delivery of Nursing Care in a Ward of a Maternity Hospital.* Unpublished Ph.D Thesis, University of Manchester.

MILES, G. (1978) Patient allocation. (Letter to the Editor). *Nursing Times,* **74,** 16, 668.

MILLER, A. (1984). Nursing process and patient care. Occasional Paper, **80,** No. 13. *Nursing Times,* June 27.

MOSER, C. A. and KALTON, G. (1971). *Survey Methods in Social Investigation.* Heineman Books (2nd Col), London.

MOULT, A., MELIA, K., HOCKEY, L. and PEMBREY, S. (1978). *Patterns of Ward Organisation.* Unpublished Report for the Leverhulme Trust Fund, Nursing Research Unit, University of Edinburgh.

MUMFORD, E. (1976). *Work Design and Job Satisfaction.* Unpublished Report, Manchester Business School.

NATIONAL NURSERY EXAMINATION BOARD (NNEB) (1981). *A Future for Nursery Nursing.* NNEB, London.

NORTON, D. (1981). The nursing process in action: the quiet revolution: introduction of the nursing process in a region. *Nursing Times,* **77,** 25, 1067–1069.

OAKLEY, A. (1979). *Becoming a Mother.* Martin Robertson and Co. Ltd.

PEMBREY, S. (1975). From work routines to patient assignment. *Nursing Times,* **71,** 45, 1768–1772.

PEMBREY, S. E. M. (1978). *The Role of the Ward Sister in the Management of Nursing: A Study of the Organisation of Nursing on an Individualised Patient Basis.* Unpublished Ph.D Thesis, University of Edinburgh.

PERKINS, E. R. (1978). *Having a Baby: An Educational Experience?* Unpublished Paper, Leverhulme Health Education Project. University of Nottingham.

PERKINS, E. (1980). *Education for Childbirth and Parenthood.* Croom Helm, London.

REDFERN, S. J. (1979). *The Charge Nurse: Job Attitudes and Occupational Stability.* Unpublished Ph.D Thesis, University of Aston.

SCOTTISH NATIONAL NURSING AND MIDWIFERY COMMITTEE (1976). A New Concept of Nursing—1. *Nursing Times,* Occasional Paper, 8th April, pp. 49–52.

STACEY, M. and HOMANS, H. (1978). The sociology of health and illness: Its present state, future prospects and potential for health research. *Sociology,* **12,** p. 281.

WALLIS, D. and COPE, D. (1980). Pay-off Conditions for Organisational Change in the Hospital Service. In: *Changes in Working Life.* Duncan, K. D., Gruneberg, M. and Wallis, D. (Eds). John Wiley and Sons, Inc., New York.

WEBB, C. (1981) Classification and framing: a sociological analysis of task-centred nursing and the nursing process. *Journal of Advanced Nursing,* **6,** 369–376.